Rockport

THE MAKING OF A TOURIST TREASURE

Eleanor Parsons

TWIN LIGHTS
PUBLISHERS, INC.

Cover design, typography, and page layout
Sharp Des!gns, Lansing, MI

ISBN 1-885435-03-7

The book cover is from an original painting by Gordan Grant, now in the
collection of the author and her husband, Story Parsons. Gordan Grant
was born in 1875 and died in 1962. He painted on Cape Ann for many
years and his paintings on nautical subjects can be seen in the
Metropolitan Museum of Art and in the Library of Congress.

Any writer of Cape Ann lore must have help every step of the way. To all of these storytellers I am forever grateful, but especially to the Sandy Bay Historical Society and its curator, Cynthia Peckham; to Erik Ronnberg for his research and original drawings of vessels in the time of John Smith; to Eddie Everett for factual information on his great-aunt, Susie Pettingill; to Pierce Sears for James Quinn photographs; and to Edward Spurlin for permission to use his map of Dogtown.

CONTENTS

Rockport

THE MAKING OF A TOURIST TREASURE

1

From the Age of Ice

CAPE ANN WAITED 40,000 YEARS FOR THE FIRST TOURIST to come and, now that curious travelers flock to this "other Cape" of Massachusetts by the hundreds of thousands, the question comes to mind, "What took them so long?"

It appears that Nature, herself, held the future of Cape Ann in her hands. It is also clear that she was in no hurry to reveal her plans. For, in the course of all those years, this remote mass of rock, later to be named Cape Ann, lay somnolent and mysterious, hidden under the greatest covering of ice the world has ever known.

Eventually, though, Nature made up her mind to unroll that incredible weight of ice, taking her time, with the ice first receding, then advancing, then receding still further, until she unveiled the second phase of her plan—with dimensions equally as astonishing as the ice—millions of tons of rock! Her lavish hand scattered giant boulders helter skelter, like pebbles on a beach.

Incredibly, Nature held in store yet a third marvel, even more awesome than the first two. The Atlantic Ocean, reaching beyond comprehension, wrapped this lonely region in a powerful embrace, and it was this last dazzling wonder, the ocean, that began to shape the Cape Ann that tourists know today.

The story of tourism on Cape Ann, of how it began and how it grew, has many parts. There are stories of mystery, of terror, of tragic shipwrecks, of brave rescues, of Old World superstitions, of strange stirrings at the bottom of the sea.

It was the endless waves creeping into uncounted and unnamed coves, and foaming surf crashing against the mass of solid rock, that carved bold sculptures of incredible beauty.

Inevitably, it was the sailor-fishermen who brought this lonely land of mystery to the attention of the civilized world. The explorers Gorges and Champlain carried back to the homeland stories of the remote shore where trees appeared to grow out of the hard grey rock, and where fish were so abundant they annoyed the fishermen who scarcely had to work to catch them. The

Vessels in the time of John Smith. Original drawing by Erik Ronnberg.

rock formations and great stretches of sandy beach held little charm for those first fishermen-adventurers. Their interests were in the great quantities of fish they could catch.

But, even as news of the new land spread, the sea continued to mutter from its depths, still grinding away at the rocks along the shore. With water and wind, Nature went right on carving out coves as methodically as a housewife prepares for guests.

For some time, however, only a few boats sailed that uncharted highway from Europe and England, and no other highway led to Cape Ann, save a footpath through the woods traveled by a few native Indians, who not only used the land for a summer retreat, but claimed ownership as well.

2

A Name for 10,000 Acres

TODAY'S TOURISTS, BY THE THOUSANDS, NOW SPIN ALONG Route 128 north from Boston, with map and guidebook at hand, but with never a thought for the man who opened this land to the rest of the world and became the most persuasive tourist agent of his time—Captain John Smith.

While present-day tourists, even with the convenience of superhighways, enter Cape Ann by its back door, John Smith, that earliest of travelers, made his bold approach by the front entrance, the Atlantic Ocean. On this ocean highway, Smith was the most resourceful of all the explorers of his day. The exploits of his youth fit perfectly into Nature's plan for Cape Ann. When a young man, he had sailed to the four quarters of the known world, was taken prisoner and held as a slave, then handed over as a prize to a princess in Turkey. To Smith's astonishment, the princess permitted him to escape from his captors. From Turkey, Smith continued searching the world's remote spots, eventually ending up helping the Jamestown Colony of Virginia.

In March 1614 he was back home in England and secured new sponsorship from the London merchants he frequently depended on. He set sail to take another look at the land he had named "New-England." There was little enthusiam for this exploration, however, and he was forced to plead for the scant two ships and the men he needed to sail them. A few daring businessmen went along, eager for the fish and gold they had heard about in so many stories.

First they anchored at Monhegan, far up the coast from the Virginia that Smith knew. There they caught large numbers of fish and whales but Smith, always the searcher and the traveler, followed the coast southward in one of the two ships. Into this shadowy region, nameless and unmapped, Smith knew that only a few travelers had ventured before him. Gosnold and Pring had sailed along this coast without stopping. Then, two years later, a third explorer, Samuel de Champlain, became the first tourist to set foot on Cape Ann.

Champlain was a thirty-seven-year-old Frenchman, somewhat more curious and observant than those who came before him. He first noticed the circle of three islands, then the headland with many small coves cutting into it. As he studied the shore line, he realized that what he saw was a "Cape of Islands," and, looking further, his searching eyes discovered figures of native Indians performing a welcome dance on the beach. He anchored his ship, went ashore, and returned their friendly greeting with his gifts of knives and biscuits. His new friends, in turn, offered grapes, nuts, and herbs. They helped him trace on a slab of wood a map of their best fishing areas, a map that John Smith never had the advantage of seeing.

So, Champlain was the first to put the cape on a map, but it was John Smith who put into words the emotion that he felt as he gazed upon Cape Ann: "the paradise of all those parts of the world" he had seen, and he had seen many wonderful, exotic sights. In fact, the three islands that formed Cape Ann reminded him of the severed heads of the three guards he had fought and outwitted when the Turkish princess gave him his freedom. Today, the islands are still known as "The Turks' Heads."

Inshore, beyond the islands, stretched the magnificent green expanse of virgin forest. Smith's notes say that this glorious garden of green amid the rock shapes could be found on no map that he knew of, nor could it boast of an official name. In his excitement he searched his mind for a name worthy of this magnificent place. At that moment he determined to christen this enchanting "paradise" in memory of the Turkish princess, and he uttered aloud the young lady's incredible name—Charatza Tragabigzanda.

Tragabigzanda! As he turned away and headed north to join his other ship, the fanciful name whirled in his head. Then, with all the other exciting details of his trip, his ships' holds full of fish, and his own crude map to show his countrymen, he hurried home to England (in 18 days) trying to awaken interest among both travelers and businessmen.

Two years elapsed before Smith was ready to embark on his next trip to New England. When, only a few days out of port, he encountered vessel trouble, he was forced to return to England for repairs. As he floundered home, a French ship waylaid him, arrested him and his crew, and threw them all into prison for some minor infraction. This delay proved crucial to John Smith's plans and, in fact, served to set the stage for the tourist industry that would one day develop on Cape Ann.

While Smith was in prison, and later, while awaiting repairs to his ship, he sorted out his jumble of notes— that was in 1616—and wrote the first tourist brochure of Cape Ann and the New England coast. Then, always alert to opportunities, he arranged to publish his papers and sell them on the streets of London and other English villages. Through all that summer, while his vessel was undergoing repairs, Smith tramped the city streets and handed out copies of his booklet, as he eagerly tried to interest merchants and voyagers in his plans. He had written a booklet of unrestrained praise of New England, and into this enthusiastic account he embedded his dream for the future.

"Of all those parts of the world that I have seen," he wrote, "could I but have means to transport a colony, I would rather live here than anywhere."

To the merchants' relentless question, "But where shall we eat?" he retorted, "If it does not maintain itself, let us starve!"

Smith's description of New England served, for many years, as the only guidebook for travelers along the New England coast. He wrote with excited enthusiasm of the delights of fishing. "Man, woman, and child," he wrote, "with a small hook and line, by angling, may take diverse sorts of excellent fish at their pleasure."

"We found there," he went on, "clams, cunners, and pinnacks, as well as beasts, such as moose, wolves, foxes, wild cats, bears, fitches, and aroughcondas."

But Smith began to realize that his small book was not persuasive enough to influence the lagging interest of London businessmen. Nevertheless, he pressed on with his arguments to anyone who would listen to him. "Let not the meanness of the word fish distaste you," he implored his countrymen, "for it will afford you as much gold as a gold mine."

In one final attempt to persuade the skeptics of his plan, he assured them, "I know a ring of gold from a grain of barley."

Eventually, Smith's descriptive words, his tales of the "New" England, and of his tongue-twisting Tragabigzanda, succeeded in attracting the attention of Ferdinando Gorges and some other London traders who, at last, began to outfit ships for the trip to Cape Ann.

By this time, however, adversity had taken its toll on John Smith. His failing health forced him to forego his long-delayed travel plans and remain in London. In the next eight years, in spite of his ailments, he persuaded crews of at least fifty ships to sail from old England to New England. Three of these ships set a course for Cape Ann.

The abundance of fish in the crystal waters of the Cape proved to be a source of discontent. Sailors began to complain of too much fish in their diet. Their boredom soon led to quarreling. In this Paradise, the bickering continued until one day a church man who had sailed with them, the Reverend John White, with exceptional insight, realized that what his companions needed was a change of diet. He sent letters back to English merchants pleading for ships "double manned and double vittaled." This was a clever plan that not only varied the fish diet, but also doubled the number of men available to fish in the summer. With this plan, half the men could remain to colonize Cape Ann, while the rest returned to England to market the fish.

As a result of the Reverend White's ingenious plan, in 1625 fourteen men remained at John Smith's Tragabigzanda, and the real destiny of the region began to unfold.

Meanwhile, King Charles I of England, who had succeeded his father James to the throne, had approved Smith's choice of a name for New England, his Tragabigzanda. Smith, however, was destined never again to see the land he so romantically named after his Turkish heroine; that rocky coast bounded by "the salt sea and ye islands," for his adventure-filled life came to an end.

Soon, a London businessman, John Mason, assumed control of the land by royal charter. There were some who questioned, though, that a king's charter could lay rightful claim to this Cape of Islands, Smith's paradise. While the merchants argued, and the seamen fished, some native Indians, sons of those who had frolicked on the beach with Champlain, filed a claim for the land. In

The signature of John English, grandson of Chief Masconomet.

a short time, however, fishermen, settlers, and Indians came to an agreement for sale of 10,000 acres. To complete the deal, they planned to meet on Christmas Day, 1700, but a violent snow storm held them all snowbound for days. When they finally met, some three weeks later, January 14, 1701, the Indians presented a deed of sale.*

This claim for justice would have satisfied John Smith as well as the Indians, but King Charles (soon to be beheaded for matters of judgment) still clung to his authority. With maternal loyalty, but without a spark of imagination, he permitted the name of his mother, Queen Anne, to replace Captain John Smith's Tragabigzanda.

---

* This historic document can be seen at Essex Institute, Salem, Massachusetts, with the distinctive signature of John English, grandson of Indian Chief, Masconomet.

3

Fishermen Set the Stage

TRAGABIGZANDA, THE NAME THAT VIBRATED WITH THE romantic spirit of John Smith, gave way to a king's whim, but travelers everywhere—merchants, adventurers, and seamen—soon recognized and accepted the name of Cape Ann. More and more ships were fitted out, but as the English boats sailed nearer, the scene of grim, grey boulders loomed ahead of them.

To the first sailor-fishermen, Cape Ann was not only a land of mystery and curiosity, but a place of fear, as well. These men, who knew all the terrors of the sea first hand, now shuddered, like children afraid of the dark, at their first glimpse of the towering trees and the rocks, both so shadowy and mysterious. Had all the rocks and all the water in the world been dumped here, they wondered? And what was hiding behind all those trees?

To add to their fears, they heard strange noises in the night—noises they could not explain away, more terrifying than anything they had ever experienced at sea. Men who remained strong in the face of sea tragedies, now trembled whenever they heard a certain wailing whistle that intensified to a howl on nights of storm and blustery winds.

The fishermen, never having heard the cry of a wolf, could only explain the wild, eerie sound as coming from the most fearsome beast they could imagine. Then, like children, they envisioned this unknown creature lurking somewhere back in the forest behind all the rocks. One man assured his companions that he had seen a wolf asleep under a tree, but no wolf appeared in daylight hours to prove his story. Later, bounties were offered for wild beasts but the fishermen, too fearful to search for them, eventually concluded that the noises emanated from some devil-like monster trying to scare them away from taking possession of the land.

In later years, scientists claimed the weird sounds came from veins in the granite. In time, as the sea continued its erosion, the veins left chasms where a loose stone might lodge and create a natural whistle. Two examples of these curiosities remain: Rafe's Chasm, near the Magnolia shore, where the sea has thundered and roared for centuries; and Chapin's Gulch, at Pigeon Cove.

Gully Point.

Weird sounds in the night and other fancies of the super-natural world fed the imaginations of these first Cape Ann settlers. Whether at sea or ashore, the mystery and the magic of their strange visions followed them. While they fished off shore by day, or when they huddled in their cabins at night, their voices lowered to a whisper as they decribed to each other the marvelous sights they had witnessed but had failed to understand: that a rainstorm and a new moon kindled salt water to flame; that a horseshoe nailed to a ship's mast brought good luck, or at least offset the bad; that sometimes Beings appeared in the darkest part of the night with whispered warnings of some dire calamity.

The "magic" that followed the fishermen appeared in as many shapes as the rocks, and often revealed itself in the form of grief or tragedy, such as when a raging storm dashed men and boats to destruction before their eyes. Those who survived catastrophes of this kind told of seeing the grieving heart of a woman in every wave. It was because of such real and recurring disasters on the sea that a ship rarely sailed into a harbor or from it without a horseshoe tacked in a conspicuous place for good luck.

One ship, carrying a crew of fishermen to Cape Ann in 1634, was caught in a violent storm but eventually inched its way, dismasted and heavily damaged, into the

The cliffs at Gap Head.

safety of a Cape Ann cove. As the ship approached the handful of curious settlers on shore, the captain pointed a shaking finger toward the broken mast. "At the height of the storm, with the ship floundering helplessly," the terrified captain told them, "I feared the worst for myself and my men." In his attempt to placate whatever sea devils he imagined were threatening them, he said he had ordered not one, but two, horseshoes, "red hot off the fire," nailed to his ship.

As the Cape Ann fishermen continued to appease their own sea devils, new ships arrived bringing even more frightening stories of crazy and mysterious happenings in other parts of the world. Old witch tales that had haunted fishermen and sailors for generations, joined the imagined monsters of the sea, to haunt them anew. Ships' crews told of long-tailed sharks they had sighted; of monsters half-woman and half-dragon; of a "witch-finder general" on the loose somewhere in the serene English countryside they had left. But it was not only England that had its witches. Stories of ghosts, snaky-haired creatures, and "black magic," were repeated and embellished throughout New England, fostered, ironically, by the same fishermen who yearned for others to join them in this lonely place.

It was in this atmosphere of mystery and superstition, of "good" and "bad" omens, that Cape Ann actually came to life. From what the fishermen knew— the sea, sailing ships, and fishing—magnified by their imaginations, evolved the character of Cape Ann. It was these men who were called upon to shape the bits and pieces of their past into a working pattern for the future of Cape Ann.

"Watch every step," the old deck-walkers cautioned. "Never move forward without first looking back."

While the cutting edge of the sea continued to sculpt the ragged stone, continued to spank the shore, continued to lash their faces with its salt spray, the Cape Ann fishermen listened to its message, and further sharpened their awareness of every motion of the sea.

Not only did these men recognize every sail when it

was still a blur on the horizon, but also perceived, with an astonishing sensitivity, every whisper of wind, the flapping of every sail, the skulling of oars, the ceaseless grinding of the sea, the constant plaintive cry of the gull over the harbor. There was no doubt that the sea was destined to set the stage for the future of Cape Ann.

As time progressed, the Massachusetts Bay Colony set aside "a psell of land in the harbor" of Gloucester on which the fishermen built a framework for drying the fish they caught. This frame was little more than a primitive scaffold made of branches, a kind of symbol for the simplicity of their lives, but it served, none-theless, as a satisfactory structure for preserving the fish for markets in England.

"It will fail," one said with foreboding. "Men have tried this before and failed. No one will come. Bad luck will follow."

In spite of the warnings, though, most of the waiting fishermen—Thomas Very, Francis Norwood, Jeffrey Parsons, and Harlakenden Symonds—knew people would come; they knew the birth of Cape Ann was at hand, and the traveler would not pass them by.

"They will come," some assured. "In time, boats will fill every cove that hugs the Cape Ann shore."

The dreams of those early fishermen, as visionary as John Smith's, soon became prophecy. The British Crown offered tax exemption, and sent an order to the distant Cape: "Let houses be built, as well as other frames and necessaries, for fish, cattle, and cows."

"Let houses be built!"

"Other frames and necessaries!"

From one pair of lips to another passed the words that rang in the future of Cape Ann, the password from old England to New England, and a new responsibility settled on the fishermen of Cape Ann.

$\mathcal{M}$

4

And the Women Came

THE FISHERMEN WERE LONELY. THEY BUILT THEIR FIRST houses, looking like one room cabins, but they always planned for the women who were to join them. A few women, with their strong religious principles, had already followed their men to Plymouth on the south shore of the bay. It was time, now, for women to join their men on Cape Ann. They came, bringing their spinning wheels, cookbooks, and Bibles, along with their personal hopes, dreams, and fears.

In a short time, Cape Ann women learned to tend the sheep and cattle, and to make shoes of cattle skins for the children. They picked blueberries by the bushel, and harvested wild raspberries, strawberries, and blackberries. Then they took time to pick the delicate pink

Wild roses on the rocks of Cape Ann.

roses that rambled in soft profusion over the hard outlines of the cold grey rock.

Still, there were long lonely hours for the women, as there had been for their men. When the men were fishing far at sea, the Cape Ann women learned to fill their hours by telling fortunes and by reading "signs" from lines in the palm of the hand. The wonders of the imagination had followed them and served both men and women.

Though women's duties kept them ashore, they were as close to the sea as were the men. Their thoughts were never far from the sea, and they found time for daily trips to the harbor to scan the waters for the fishing

Drying fish.

boat most familiar to them. Over the sound of splashing waves, they shouted words of greeting, not only to bolster their own courage, but to cheer the men as well. Then, when the men reached shore, the women were there to assist in laying out the fish to dry on their hand-made frames.

The drying process, called "making" the fish, took from four to ten days depending on changes of weather. If the sun's rays were too hot, the fish burned. So they learned to cover the fish with pieces of sailcloth or to shade them with green boughs during the heat of the day. At night, both men and women workers removed the drying fish from the frames and tossed them, skin upward, in heaps on the ground. The next morning the fish would be spread again on the frames or "flakes" for further drying.

When their men fished far off shore, the women would take the children to the harbor, where they built bonfires as signals to guide their men home through the dark nothingness of the ocean. They taught the children how to pile on wood to keep the fires burning as long as necessary, sometimes all night, to guide their men home safely. Great storms blowing off the ocean often brought entire families to the harbor for many hours of anxious waiting. At such times, the women could only watch and pray for the fishermen so far out to sea that their vessels, if they could see them at all, resembled children's toy boats.

Ironically, if a storm ended in tragedy and death, the widows often ended up with more opportunity than when their husbands were alive. Mary Norwood Gamage, for example, obtained work as a sexton in the new church. Such work was usually offered to keep a widow off the general dole, although her meager earnings were less than the church would have paid for the same services provided by a man.

Women were often more regular in church attendance and, at one time, church records listed as members twenty-one males and forty-nine females. Men,

The old log cabin, the oldest house in Rockport Village.

nevertheless, were true to their faith, especially when fortified by their superstitions. They rarely fished on Sunday, and most men would have jumped overboard rather than drive a nail on the Sabbath.

The early women of Cape Ann developed many talents, and they were no less determined than the men to use their skills for the advantage of the entire community. After Mary Gamage performed her church duties, she often was called upon to officiate "in the medical line among her sex." For these necessary services as a "skilled practitioner of the healing art," the town paid her a few extra dollars.

In 1637, Isabel Babson came from Salem to Gloucester with her small son, James. She served as midwife, physician, and nurse. The town officials so appreciated her "usefulness" that they deeded to her one of Cape Ann's most fertile tracts of farm land.

Although it was to be many decades before artists came to Cape Ann, another skill soon became evident among the early settlers. Mary Trichor Brown learned to barber. Many men considered this a "peculiar skill," but Mary Brown thought so highly of her art that she taught it to her daughter. Becky Brown was thought to be of superior intelligence, not only because of her special skill, but also because of her ability to carry on a lively conversation with men. More important than either of these skills, however, was her interest in drawing pictures. She covered the walls of her barber shop with sketches of birds and flowers, as well as humorous anecdotes and poetry. Becky Brown was probably Cape Ann's first artist!

Women were rarely recorded in Cape Ann history, but they were so important to its development that they cannot be overlooked in its story. One woman gained a lasting fame simply by making the first cup of coffee on Cape Ann. Another, Ruth Miller, received the dubious honor of being the first woman to occupy the new workhouse built for those with no means of support. This structure was a 12-by-14-foot rectangle built in 1719. Mary Perkins was yet another woman who struggled in

The Old Gott House, Pigeon Cove.

Cape Ann's early days. She ran a tavern after her husband died at sea, leaving her with a large family of children to support.

These strong female characters helped shape Cape Ann, but it must be acknowledged that some, alas, were great trials to their husbands. Anna Pecker, for example, was a traveler from Haverhill who had married the Reverend Samuel Chandler. It was rare for a Cape Anner to look for a wife from "off the place," and the Reverend probably should have had some second thoughts before taking the step. For Anna proved to be unfaithful to him, and he complained to his friends that she annoyed him "in unusual ways!" Eventually, the harassed clergyman lamented in public that his Haverhill wife must have "either a disordered intellect or a perverse heart."

Josiah Cheever was another disillusioned young man who lost his heart over a disastrous love affair. He fell in love with the church deacon's beautiful daughter, but in the end she scorned him and ran off with his father.

For the most part, though, Cape Ann women lived up to their reputation of being hard workers, self-reliant, and independent. In spite of their deprivations and in spite of the custom of being segregated from male parishioners in their church, and sent to the east gallery of the new meeting house in 1700, they found ways to get by. Isabel Babson, for example, managed to leave a sizable estate of $25, something for other women to dream about for themselves. When all else failed them, they had one place to go for consolation. It was at the harbor that early women of Cape Ann found their courage to keep going. For the harbors, where families came to work and to watch, were the lifelines of Cape Ann.

"Harbors are human," said one wise old fisherman. "And they are something like women. They have their times for dainty and delicate attire. To know them you must study them, under daylight, at sunrise and at sunset, under the full harvest moon, at low tide and at high tide; in a storm and after the storm is over. Then you will find some mood to admire, new beauty come to light. Our harbor sulks sometimes, as a dog day's fog hangs over it; as it shares its favors with many craft."

In Cape Ann's first hundred years, it shared its favors with seven hundred "newcomers," not really tourists at this point, but usually wayfarers who had no idea that they were visiting Paradise.

5

Then the Pirates

AS THE DECADES OF THE SEVENTEENTH CENTURY SLIPPED by, an increasing number of strangers wandered up from Plymouth or down from the northern wilderness. Almost unnoticed, the crude shelters built by the early fishermen changed into houses large enough to accommodate these visiting strangers, as well as their own growing families.

By mid-century, more and more boats sought shelter in the secluded coves. But now, as gradually as the houses had appeared, a new and unexpected menace threatened the entire Cape—pirate ships crowded the waters off the coast.

For a generation, Cape Ann had known only friendly fishing boats, but now pirate crews became unwelcome visitors whose ships filled the coves and inlets, waving their flags in jaunty defiance. For one hundred years the Jolly Roger, black flag of the Barbary pirates, waved over Cape Ann coves and islands, while the command to "sling him overboard" echoed in Sandy Bay.

Ironically, these unwelcome strangers, highwaymen of the sea, were nearly all British buccaneers from the fishermen's own homeland. Because of this close relationship, they were tolerated for a century, until English law took over and authorized piracy cases to be tried in colonial courts.

This thievery on the seas flourished along the New England coast, not because the fishermen had money or other treasures, for they had none of these, but because their coves offered shelter. No one was immune to the assaults.

John Smith wrote in 1630 that "in all seas there are some pirates," and in 1704, "nine or eleven" pirate ships sailed with a bold defiance into Gloucester harbor. Cape Anners knew little of these unwanted travelers, but stories of their deeds were heard around the world. In some ways they admired the daring strangers and, at times, even approved of what they did. But they always feared them and looked upon them with curiosity and suspicion.

Names such as Francis Drake, John Hawkins, Edward "Blackbeard" Teach, even Columbus, were familiar pirate names recognized around the world. One of the more colorful figures, Aristotle Tottle, was known as the "timid pirate." Another was Montbars, the Exterminator. Still another was Roc the Brazilian, and yes, there were two women pirates, Anne Bonney and Mary Read. Anne Bonney was an Irish girl who followed her lover, Calico Jack, around the seven seas. Her friend, Mary Read, had been reared as a boy in the Carolinas, and she took to her career with the stout-hearted abandon of her male companions.

The three pirates best known to Cape Ann, however, were the three Johns—John Nott, John Quelch, and John Phillips—and it was this gang that finally met its match on Cape Ann. For six months they had harassed Cape Ann fishermen, plundering the New England coast, and causing alarm and fear at the loss of so many ships. The gang had seized thirty-four vessels, four of them from Gloucester, before the fishermen found the opportunity to strike back at them.

Captain Andrew Harraden of Annisquam, and his crew of fishermen, had all but finished construction of a new sloop and they had launched it for a trial sail in the harbor. While they were all busily working on the ship, John Phillips and his pirate crew waylaid them and ordered them to complete the ship's carpentry under guard.

The fishermen had no intention of giving up their new vessel without a struggle, and they remained alert for any sign that the pirates were momentarily off guard. At noon, with their unwelcome guests relaxed, the quick-witted Captain Harraden signaled his men, and using the carpenter's tools they had at hand, they overpowered the gang of pirates and took them captive.

With the ship once more in hand, the owner sailed back into Annisquam harbor in triumph, with the head of Pirate John Phillips swinging from the mast. Other members of the pirate crew were hanged from trees on an island in the Annisquam River, and in the ears of John Nott echoed the command of Harraden's men to "sling him over-board!"

From time to time, as in this instance, pirates succeeded in landing on Cape Ann shores, and, though their voices had been stilled for a time, certain signs of these unwelcome guests remained.

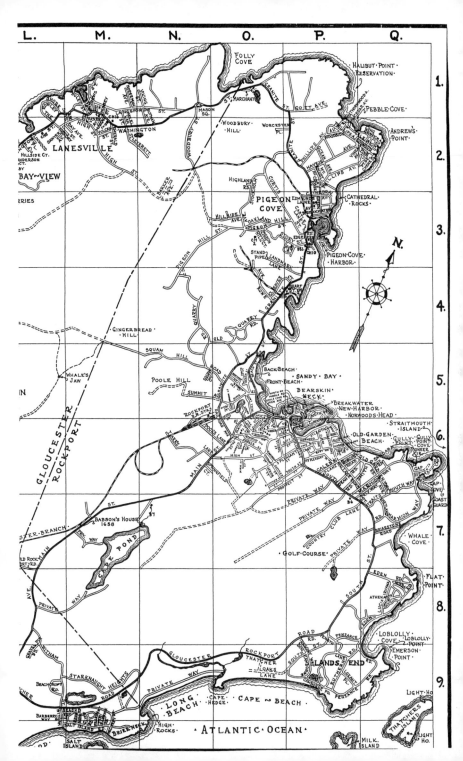

6

Found: A Pot of Real Gold

AT FIRST THERE WAS NO REAL PROOF THAT PIRATES HAD ever actually come ashore at Gully Cove, but there was just enough evidence to arouse the curiosity of thirteen-year-old Caleb Norwood.

For many years Gully Cove, behind Straitsmouth Island, had been a favorite shelter for pirate ships, protected from storms, as well as enemies. It was the best cove around Cape Ann for unloading the fish to dry. Naturally, local fishermen, as well as visitors, favored this cove.

Joshua Norwood was one of the fishermen who had bought land near Gully Cove. He had moved from Pigeon Cove to Attleboro, and then returned to Cape Ann with his wife, Elizabeth, and their fifteen children. Caleb, the last of their offspring, was born in 1739.

Caleb had already bought a small fishing boat, called a wherry. In order to pay for his boat he worked on the farm of his neighbor, Francis Pool. The mast for his boat had cost him nothing. He had cut, trimmed, and peeled off the bark from a pine sapling, and his father had taught him how to step it for a mast. The sail had been cut down from a piece of another sail that he had rescued from an old derelict.

Caleb often dreamed of sailing out into the bay where pirate ships anchored, but each time he gathered his courage the black flag seemed to whip its message of defiance and sail off toward the horizon. The young man worked every daylight hour, but at night there was little to entertain a thirteen-year-old boy, except to squint through the cracks of the logs of the family cabin, and hope for something to move in the dark void of a Cape Ann night.

The very thought of pirates so close offshore kept the family in fear for months at a time. One night, Caleb peered into the darkness and saw two figures stumbling over the rocks and carrying a shadowy object from the cove toward Pool's field. Excitement stirred within him. He crept into bed, his heart pounding violently, while his mind plotted one wild scheme after another. He had to know what those two pirates had hidden in the field.

In Caleb's mind there was never a doubt that the dim figures were pirates.

The next day, Caleb went to work as usual to plow the neighboring field of Francis Pool. With the pirates never far from his mind, he looked with suspicion on every mound of earth, on every stone he turned over.

Suddenly, Caleb dropped to his knees in the plowed furrow and began to dig his bare hands into the soft meadow mud. Caleb's eager, searching fingers almost immediately felt the hard lid of an iron receptacle. His heart pounded as it had done, the previous night. Working fast, he tugged at the heavy coffer, but the mud held it as if it had no intention of giving up its secret. At last, he realized he must have help. He called to his employer across the field and Francis Pool needed only a hasty glance to rouse his own curiosity. Together, Caleb Norwood and Francis Pool succeeded in prying open the cover and now, quivering with excitement, they gazed in speechless awe at an iron bucket full of gold bars.

The true value of the treasure they found that day has often been questioned, but discovered recently among old papers in the Sandy Bay Historical Society is a handwritten note, dated 1772. "We have good reason to believe," the note states, "that Caleb Norwood found buried near the Gully at Gully Point from $7,000 to $10,000 worth of gold." In any case, Caleb Norwood and Francis Pool soon became men of great wealth for their day. Caleb not only paid for his wherry, but in later years the Norwood family built at least six of the finest homes in Sandy Bay (now Rockport); houses so well constructed that they remain habitable to this day.

News of finding the fabulous hidden cache of gold spread outside Sandy Bay as fast as sunshine dispels a morning fog. For the first time, crowds of curious travelers flocked to Cape Ann, and the fishermen, always seeking companionship, welcomed the questioning strangers. The Norwoods and the Pools even went so far as to boast that the Barbary pirates had singled out their own sequestered cove for hiding the treasure. Then, wisely or not, Cape Anners went one step further. With unprecedented hospitality, they granted permission to outsiders to come and search their coves— but with certain limitations.

"Come in the dark of night," they whispered in a furtive warning, "and don't talk too much!"

Then, in the same hushed undertones their fathers and grandfathers had used when they spoke of wolf cries and witches, they cautioned: "The mysterious Hand that holds the bail on the pot of gold yanks it away from the noisy ones!"

As far as the fishermen were concerned, the old magic and the mystery still clung to Cape Ann, and still breathed life into her veins. As they watched, listened, and searched, more strangers drifted in like the tide. Neither strangers nor fishermen were able to dismiss from their minds the echo of pirate voices, while the chance of even more fabulous riches, lying unclaimed beneath a Cape Ann boulder, continued to tantalize their imaginations.

7

A Hesitant Welcome

THE NEW TOURISTS, MANY NOW TRAVELING BY LAND instead of by sea, hiked to Cape Ann through the wood's path as native Indians had before them. There was still only one land route into Cape Ann, and the ancient trail wound all the way from Salem to the Cape, following the coast where other fishermen had settled.

In order to reach the most easterly parts of Cape Ann, these tourists had to cross the Annisquam River by ferry, at a point known as Trynall Cove, where the river cut Cape Ann almost in half. Only one narrow sand bar prevented the northern half, Sandy Bay, from being a complete island.

From the time the first sailors had taken possession of the land, all this shoreline north of Salem was called Cape Ann Ferry or Cape Ann-Side. An early English law had established that "all a man sailed by or saw was his own," and any man who made a new discovery "held exclusive rights to acquire soil from a native." It was by this early, all-embracing law that the first adventurous seamen claimed the shore property. New owners then proceeded to divide the lots for farming and cut thatch for their houses as they had in England. It was along this shore, too, that the waters of Massachusetts Bay clasped hands with Ipswich Bay to form the arms that encircled Cape Ann.

Although these two bodies of water were protective and very desirable for fishing, the sand bar at Trynall Cove was another matter. It became, in fact, Cape Ann's introduction to traffic problems. Though traffic of that day was minimal, the ferry traffic, such as it was, had to be detoured to the deeper water of the bay. Consequently, this insignificant strip of sand became the subject of a controversy that persisted for decades.

"If we could but cut through that sand bar," the fishermen argued, "ships could then sail from Ipswich Bay, at the north of the cape, straight through to Gloucester harbor, without going all the way around the outer cape. With this cut we could avoid delay, as well as the risk of storms."

In 1638, Governor Endicott sent three men from Salem to Cape Ann to consider the fishermens' proposal. But the study ended in disappointment. The three-man committee concluded that the work was too trivial for the attention of the busy Colonial government.

The fishermen took their disappointment, and their arguments, to the local town government of Gloucester. For another five years they argued the need for a connection with Cape Ann. At last, Gloucester voted to permit someone to "cut through the beach, and to maintain it, and to have the benefit of it to himself and his heirs forever, giving the inhabitants of the town free passage."

The trouble with this decision was that no one wanted to do the work! Eventually, it was another minister, as it had been in the early days of their settlement, who offered to help them out. The Reverend Richard Blynman, from Wales, who now lived nearby and desperately needed the money, agreed to build the canal.

The structure for the canal was simple: two parallel walls of rock, narrowed at the bottom, sloping outward at the top, and just wide enough to allow passage of a small shallop. Of course, once the sand bar was cut and the retaining wall built, there was no way, except by ferry, for the increasing number of foot travelers to cross into Gloucester.

Consequently, Blynman and his crew went on to build a bridge. Crude though it was, the bridge was an ingenious structure, for it was designed to swing on a pivot. In this way it would accommodate both foot travelers and boats.

With the project completed, the cut and its bridge severed the Cape in almost equal sections. Occasionally, someone forgot to swing the bridge back after opening it, and this inconvenience finally made it necessary for Gloucester officials to levy a fine of six shillings on these absent-minded travelers.

The bridge and canal worked well for fifty years— until disaster struck! In 1704, a wind storm and exceptionally high tides swept back all the sand that had once formed the sand bar, making the crossing as useless as it had been in the first place. Again, travel to Cape Ann was almost at a standstill. After some delay, the fishermen overcame their frustration and once more cleared away the sand so travel could resume. Nature and her ocean, however, still were in charge. Within twenty years another storm repeated all the damage of the first storm.

By this time, a new owner had taken over the property from Blynman, but both the new owner and Gloucester officials had become so discouraged that they refused to accept further responsibility for clearing away the sand again. Now, travel to Cape Ann was all but stopped. As in the beginning, a few travelers came by boat, but the cut could be used very little for commercial purposes and the structure was essentially abandoned for another hundred years. At one point in this period, Cape Ann was considered to be so unattractive to travelers that the population changed not at all in twenty-five years.

Meanwhile, someone with renewed courage laboriously cleared away the sand, and once again travelers resumed use of the cut. As early as 1759, talks also began about building a new bridge of more permanent construction. Yet, for three hundred years, (until Route 128 was completed in 1953) the cut served as the only land route to that section of Cape Ann east of the Annisquam River. The cut, and its primitive bridge, was Cape Ann's first faltering effort to accommodate the traveling stranger.

8

A Silent Visitor

MORE TRAVELERS MANAGED TO FIND THEIR WAY OVER the cut, always dreaming, no doubt, of that intriguing, yet elusive pot of gold. But some Cape Anners were already having misgivings about the newcomers who were often noisy and troublesome. It was not long before some of them stayed to take up residence and to fish. The worried officials of Gloucester foresaw awkward situations ahead. The apprehensive officials lost no time in writing into their records certain restrictions regarding the six-acre grants of land that were parceled out to all men when they reached the age of twenty-one.

"Sell if you must," the town officials warned, "but don't sell to a stranger unless you have to."

Squabbling on land. Thievery at sea. Was this the road Nature had planned for Cape Ann?

The strangers came and went, not always welcome now but, nevertheless, spreading the word about the mysterious cape. Some arrived by the customary method of transportation, a sailboat; others came by way of the ferry; still others struggled over the cut. One visitor, daring and adventurous, chose to swim into Gloucester harbor!

For seventeen days this alien "visitor" swam about in Gloucester harbor, sightseeing as sailors had before him, while curious citizens stared back at this strangest visitor of all—a sea serpent! Every day hundreds of curiosity seekers, Cape Anners, as well as "outsiders," flocked to the harbor hoping to catch a glimpse of the odd creature. "What was he doing?" they asked each other. Had he sought shelter in their coves, like the pirates? Or had he perhaps chased a school of herring to their door?

"He's a great brown snake," one onlooker described the creature, "perhaps eighty feet long, the length of a large sailing vessel, but not much larger around than a good sized man!"

"And he's shy," another added.

Stories of this latest tourist multiplied as fast as the news of pirates and the cache of gold. As word spread, a committee came from Boston to question "reliable" witnesses, those whose reputation upheld their statements: clergymen, sea captains, and town officials.

The silent visitor departed as mysteriously as he had arrived, but Cape Anners could not forget. While many questioned that a real sea serpent had sought shelter in a Cape Ann harbor, or even that one existed at all, the committee from Boston, after asking a list of twenty-five questions, reported, "We are not skeptical." Moreover, their investigations concluded that Cape Ann and Norway, because of their rocky coastlines, were the two areas most frequented by this sea traveler.

Incidentally, mermaids were even rarer than sea serpents, but one day a Gloucester fisherman said he saw one at closer range than he would have wished.

"We almost captured her," he said of this astonishing swimmer. "She was clinging to the gunwhales." Their superstitions and fear aroused the crew to panic, and they shoved their boat away from the captivating sea creature they imagined was following them.

Another story tried to prove the existence of sea maidens. "One day," the story teller related, "a beautiful creature surfaced, with her long blond hair streaming over her shoulders. She smiled with white teeth gleaming, and flashed the torso of a young sea witch. But the lower half of her body," he assured his listeners, "was startlingly like a fish, with scales, fins, and a tail."

While the sea promoted no end of myths and unforgettable horror stories; at the same time, it nurtured stories of romance and young love, and the point of land where the ocean washes over the rocks at Hoop Pole Cove gave rise to one particularly poignant love story.

9

A Bridegroom without Ceremony

AS THE NUMBER OF HOUSES INCREASED FOR THOSE TOUR-
ists who settled on Cape Ann, weddings became more
frequent, as well. In the earliest days of Cape Ann,
marriages were often arranged for convenience, and
almost as soon as one spouse died, another filled the
space of the absent one. If several widows were left as
the result of a shipwreck, most of them lost no time in
finding another fisherman, probably a widower, to help
bring up the children. One Cape Ann marriage, however,
attests to true love as exciting as any novel.

This early romance developed just west of Andrews
Point, at Hoop Pole Cove, one of the tiniest and most
secluded coves on the northeast corner of Cape Ann,
often called The Tip of Cape Ann, since this is the
spit of land that reaches farthest into the Atlantic. At

this Point, Mary Andrews grew to womanhood. Mary's grandfather, William Andrews, had traveled from Ipswich to the Halibut Point-Andrews Point-Hoop Pole Cove area about 1701, the year Cape Ann was purchased from Indian owners. William was unmarried at the time, but his sisters, Margaret and Elizabeth, were already settled there. Margaret had married Samuel Gott, who now sold to William, his brother-in-law, eighteen acres "by the cove usually called Hoop Pole Cove."

William's other sister, Elizabeth, had married Joshua Norwood who, at age twenty-one, had received his grant of land according to Colonial law, and now owned 325 acres that included a modest dwelling, later to be known as a "witch house." (Note: It was their fifteenth child, Caleb, who found the pirate gold at Gully Cove.)

At the time William acquired his land at Andrews Point, he was twenty-nine years old. Within a dozen years he could count a total of fifty-five acres, enough to enable him to marry Elizabeth Curtis of Ipswich. In later years, when the estate of William and Elizabeth was settled, the land was divided among their three children, and son Jonathan's share included all of Andrews Point.

It was there, in the atmosphere of a "witch" house, the discovery of pirate gold, and acres of uncut forest, that Jonathan's daughter, Mary Andrews, grew into a beautiful young woman. Mary was a dreamer and a romantic, but in the Pigeon Cove of those days there was nothing at all for a young girl to view but trees and sky and ocean. Trees and tides were far more plentiful than young men.

As Mary grew older her day dreams became more and more imaginative until, at times, she saw visions as clearly as her fishermen forebears. Sometimes, when she strolled along the sea shore, she believed she heard voices that seemed to rise out of the surf. One of her private fantasies recurred again and again; she dreamed of a handsome young man, dressed in a uniform of scarlet and gleaming gold, who appeared out of the waves. She imagined he had come from the other side of the ocean to seek her as his wife. Mary's dream was so real that she assured her family that she had actually talked with the young man, that he had promised to return to her, and that they had pledged their love to last forever.

Mary persisted in clinging to her fanciful dream in spite of her parents' dismay. They held no such notions and had aspirations for their daughter to marry a handsome young fisherman dressed in a guernsey jacket. Against all arguments, however, Mary clung to her dreams, spurning all offers of marriage, until her worried parents feared she was close to becoming an old maid of twenty-five.

Meanwhile, Mary had another dream, equally as real to her, but less joyful. She dreamed the same young man lay severely injured and near death on Andrews Point. This vision became so real to her that she went daily to Hoop Pole Cove to search for her imaginary lover.

One day in May, when a warm spring breeze blew in from the ocean, the dream appeared again, so real that it captured her mind completely. Forgetting her usual household duties, the breakfast dishes, the sewing, the stirring of pots at the fireplace, she set off on her favorite walk through the woods to Hoop Pole Cove. Along the way, she admired the dainty white bloom of the shad bush, at the same time listening for the special secrets of the ancient forest that sloped to the edge of the sea.

Mary's thoughts wandered to the young man of her dreams and then, suddenly, there he was. He was lying in the wet sand, still and pale, with his handsome head resting on one arm. His once trim uniform was torn and soiled with salt water and seaweed. Mary dropped to her knees and wiped the pale face with the hem of her skirt, peering anxiously for some sign of life. Miraculously, he stirred, opened his eyes, and gazed in wonder at the pretty girl kneeling on the sand beside him. When he tried to rise, Mary helped him to his feet, placed her arm around his shoulders for support, and led the stranger to her home through the woodsy path.

Six months later, November 5, 1778, Mary Andrews became the bride of Stephen Knutsford. For a long time, Stephen kept to himself the secret of his past, or what accident of fate had brought him to Andrews Point. His uniform indicated that he had been in the service of the British, and British law still reached out its arms to claim its citizens. Mary's parents accepted Stephen's assurances that he came from a titled Danish-English family, and that he had been a soldier with General Burgoyne when the surrender came at Saratoga, October 17, 1777.

Eventually, the complete story unfolded. When General George Washington permitted Burgoyne to return to England, Stephen Knutsford had been assigned to the returning vessel. Enroute home, the ship became fogbound off Straitsmouth Island, at the southern tip of Cape Ann. Officer Knutsford, weakened and ill from his war service, and with the ship tossing in rolling surf, somehow fell overboard. Unnoticed by his crewmen, he began to swim toward shore, a distance of about four miles, where Mary Andrews found his exhausted form on that fateful day in May.

Stephen and Mary had eight children, but Stephen, having been educated in a family of nobility, was unprepared for the primitive living conditions of a fisherman on Cape Ann. Instead of becoming a fisherman to support his large family, he became a school teacher at Pigeon Cove. Stephen Knutsford, it seemed, possessed special skills almost unknown among Cape Ann fishermen of that time. Stephen could read and write. Furthermore, he could "rhyme," and as a teacher, he soon earned the respect and admiration of his Pigeon Cove neighbors.

Though Stephen Knutsford had literally been tossed up by the sea as so much flotsam, this visitor from the sea, as well as Mary Andrew's visions, only added to the ocean mysteries of Cape Ann. With the ocean endlessly at work washing in strange creatures, always molding, carving, rearranging, the rocks of Cape Ann began to assume that special significance foretold thousands of years earlier. Were all those rocks dumped here for a purpose?

10

Names Are Significant

NATURE WAS NOT YET READY TO REVEAL HER SECRET plan for the rocks of Cape Ann but they remained an appealing curiosity. In time, the rocks began to develop what can only be called personalities. Many of them even acquired names that became as significant to the fishermen as naming their boats and their children. From the days when John Smith's Tragabigzanda took the name of an English queen, to the time when pirates had distinctive, whimsical names, rocks captured the fancy of fishermen.

Whenever Cape Anners gathered around the coves to talk of fishing and the weather, naming rocks, boats, and children was a popular pastime. With many families like the Norwoods, raising twelve or fifteen children, it is not surprising that at times some parents, with little imagination, ran out of names and gave the same name to two of their children. For some families, however, names appear to have satisfied some creative urge, resulting in highly imaginative and unusual names for their offspring.

For example, first settlers Grace and Richard Tarr, while awaiting the birth of their first child in 1722, must have searched their well-thumbed Bible from Genesis to Revelation before pausing in the Book of Chronicles to come up with the important-sounding name of Hazelelponi!

In a later generation, Mr. and Mrs. Samuel Webber named their twins Patience and Waitstill. Then, among the fifteen children of Samuel Hopkins and his two wives, Hannah and Mary, were three daughters named Mercy, Patience, and Experience.

One young girl survived her unusual name to grow up and become a bride. On a May day, she traveled from Gloucester to Ipswich to make her marriage legal, for there was no marriage "magistrate" available in Gloucester. The bride's name was Remember Jones.

Not all early settlers, however, wasted their time in creating fanciful names. Following close on the heels of Richard Tarr, John Pool came to help construct early wharves, then to build the first frame house, the first mill, the first vessel. John, it can be noted, was more of

The Whale's Jaw.

a carpenter than a fisherman, and he was a shameless romantic, as well. He married four times in the span of five years, and fathered nine children. While Elizabeth, his third wife, was on her death bed, he already had his eyes on pretty Abigail Ballard, a tourist from Lynn, and he persuaded Abigail to become engaged on short notice. News of the engagement was posted in May, but then Abigail had some second thoughts about becoming the fourth wife of a fifty-one-year-old carpenter with seven children—especially since his third wife was still alive—and she sent John packing.

Meanwhile, when Elizabeth conveniently died in July, Abigail reconsidered and sent John the message he had been waiting for, that she would welcome his return to her. John returned forthwith and, romantic fellow that he was, insisted that their first son should be named to memorialize their great love. They named the boy Return!

While the choice of names for the children stretched the imagination of Cape Ann fishermen and their wives, the naming of boats was probably of equal importance to them. These names, too, were used over and over again like heirlooms.

Though owners of boats frequently used their own names, often the name of a mother, wife, or daughter graced the prow of a new vessel. Sometimes, too, they favored "sea" names such as *Neptune's Bride*, *Dolphin*, or *Nautilus*. True to their old beliefs, though, they often chose a "lucky" name to honor an earlier vessel, one that had already withstood north Atlantic storms, or had brought in a good catch of fish.

In the early days, few fishermen could afford vessels of their own. In 1775, a mere fifty families had settled on the eastern edge of Cape Ann (then called Sandy Bay, now Rockport), and only four of those owned fishing schooners. Those four "bankers" bore the names of Morning Star, Rising Sun, Friendship, and Little John. The bankers of that day, incidentally, were not what the name implies today—men who handle money. Bankers were schooners that carried a crew of fishermen to fish off the Grand Banks, near Nova Scotia and Newfoundland. The Grand Banks is a range of underwater mountains lying between North America and Europe. This range runs nearly north and south for about 1200 miles, while the width and height vary like mountains above the sea. The Cape Ann "bankers," it was said, were as close to real money as most of the fishermen ever came.

In addition to naming their boats and their children, the families of Cape Ann fishermen also highly valued the rocks that so influenced their lives. Although always a curiosity, no one yet had any idea what to do with all that rock.

As time went by, some of the rocks, inevitably, became landmarks of great interest. One rock, discovered by a farmer as he followed Driftwood Lane to the sea, attracted almost as much attention as the sea serpent. The rock was of no unique shape, but by some accident of nature, it was singled out as a rock that jingled! When a passer-by touched it lightly with a forefinger, the rock tinkled like a bell.

Another stone became an object of interest because of a spectral visitor. A woodcutter on Dogtown Common awoke from a nap like Rip Van Winkle, and imagined he saw a ghostly figure among the rocks. He related that as he wakened he heard soft music and saw a figure clad in a flowing white robe, descending a gold ladder that appeared to hang from a cloud. When the spectral form reached the bottom rung of the glittering ladder, the music ceased and the figure vanished. The woodsman, in awe by his experience, began to chisel out his initials in a rock. When he had finished his rough carving he reverently placed the stone upon a higher rock to look like a pulpit, and there it remained for years for travelers to admire. This curiosity, named the Vision Stone, has been preserved as a museum piece.

The most celebrated rock of all, though, became known as The Whale's Jaw. This was an enormous boulder in the heart of Cape Ann, that once resembled the sea creature from which it was named. Time, weather, and vandalism, however, have crumbled the familiar stone to a shape that is no longer recognizable as a whale. Nevertheless, its shattered sections remain as a favorite picnic spot, as well as a resting place for annual blueberry pickers.

In addition to these landmarks, there are the less obvious "stone seats," mill stones used for the early sawmills, and numerous "rocking rocks" that could be moved, like the Jingle Bell Rock, with the touch of a finger. While naming rocks appeared to lend a certain dignity to some of Cape Ann's boulders, many fishermen, as well as visitors, still believed that special stones marked spots where pirates had concealed additional treasure. Still, uses of the rock were limited and the great treasure of ledge that lay under Cape Ann remained undiscovered, as silent and mysterious as the glacier had left it.

11

The Fosters of Dogtown

THE LEDGE OF ROCK UNDER CAPE ANN REMAINED UN-used, for the most part unwanted, and, certainly, unrecognized as the treasure it was later to become. Nature still waited for the time to use the rocks she had dumped there. She procrastinated for another hundred years.

Meanwhile, as Cape Ann waited for the drama of rock to unfold, history wrote a unique story—a story that became a kind of sidelight to the larger history of this remarkable Cape. From all sides of the Cape, this great wasteland of rock sloped upward and inward away from the shore. In this heartland, literally the throbbing heart of Cape Ann, lay a thousand acres of wild land and boulders (about one-tenth of all of Cape Ann), barren, forbidding, mystical. So far as anyone had yet discovered, its only use was to feed cattle in a common pasture. Of all the unsettled places on Cape Ann, here on this common land it was easy to believe in the ancient magic. Here, no one tried to explain the mysteries that pervaded the primitive region.

The fear of witches had never left the Cape Ann mind, nor had the fear of enemies offshore. In this century, pirates had barely disappeared from the horizon when the American Revolution brought to Cape Ann a new enemy, their own former countrymen. When Cape Anners first heard the news of guns at Lexington, they were already alert to British vessels, well armed and hovering off their coast. Just as pirates had sought shelter in their coves only a few decades before, now British vessels, seeking contraband from their antagonists, sailed too close to shore for watchers to ignore the peril.

With this new fear, Cape Ann fishermen and farmers alike were soon on their way to Boston to put an end to the outrage. Before they departed, however, some men moved their families back from the harbor, to the comparative safety of that common pastureland.

The isolated Common, though desolate and forbidding, nevertheless provided the means for women and children to raise vegetables and to watch over grazing cattle. Not only would families remain relatively

The road to "Dogtown" and across Cape Ann from Gloucester to Rockport.

safe from sea dangers, but also they could feed themselves while the fishermen were absent, or if they failed to return at all.

Josiah Foster was one of the fishermen who decided to move his family to the Common, and in the half light of a June morning he was on his way to his new home. With his feet clad in clumsy boots of hand-sewn cattle skins, Josiah strode ahead of his young daughter with a cat-like grace born of walking decks of sailing vessels.

Eight-year-old Dorcas, motherless since her mother had died of the dreaded consumption, followed close behind her father on the narrow footpath that led from

Gloucester harbor, upward toward the Common. Her bare feet spanked the cold wet earth and now and then she grasped the leg of a wooden stool her father carried on his back.

From the high land of the Common, in the early light of dawn, the entire coast north to New Hampshire was discernible, as was the six miles of rocky coastline that hugged in Sandy Bay. From the great expanse of ocean, wild geese flew over the Common on their way across Ipswich Bay from Plum Island.

Josiah paid no attention to the familiar sight. Already he was weary, for, in addition to his back pack, he carried his oars and his rifle, and on his chest he balanced a lumpy bundle, all the worldly goods the two possessed. Under the weight, he bent into the upgrade as an older man might have done. But his step was the decisive step of a man not yet thirty years old. It was moving day for the Fosters, father and daughter.

"Have we finished the house, Father?"

Josiah turned his head for the mist to blow his words to the ears of his small daughter. "Enough done for you to live in, Dorcas. You'll be safe here while I'm gone."

His words were of little comfort. Dorcas shivered as the dampness cut through the dress that she had already washed to a faded thinness. "I felt safe at the harbor, Father." Her words were a half whisper and she was not sure her father had heard her. The long dress slapped her ankles, keeping her legs warm but her feet had lost all feeling in them. Safe? Safe from what?

"All these rocks, Father. Easter Carter says witches live behind them."

The dawn haze drifted over Sandy Bay, making the ancient boulders look like head stones in some crowded cemetery. The jagged stones, many looming above her head, blended into the half dawn light. Dorcas was too young to appreciate the artistry of the stones, but old enough to recognize the fear that she felt far down at the bottom of her heart.

Josiah did not laugh at his daughter's fears. Perhaps witches did live behind the rocks. He was not so sure of that himself. When the two reached the top of the rise, Josiah paused at the stone wall to rest and catch his breath.

"Good old Parson Winslow will be here, close by," he told Dorcas. "He takes on the devil so he'll know what to do with witches." Then, to reassure her, he added, "And Easter Carter, too. If anyone knows what to do with witches, Easter does. She's just across the path and she can hear as if she was in the next room."

Josiah rested his oars and his rifle against the stone wall. Then, shifting his back and front packs to a better balance, he climbed over the wall and turned

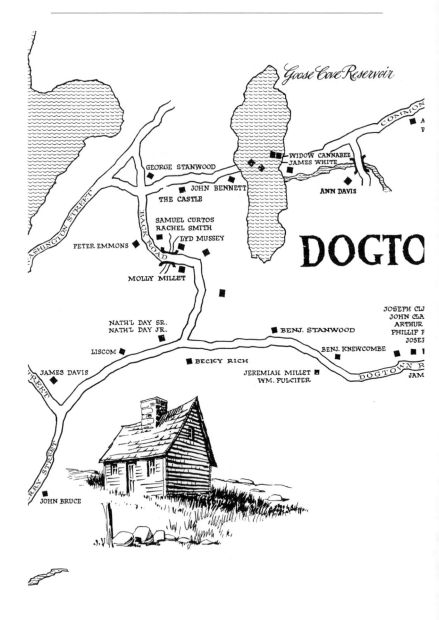

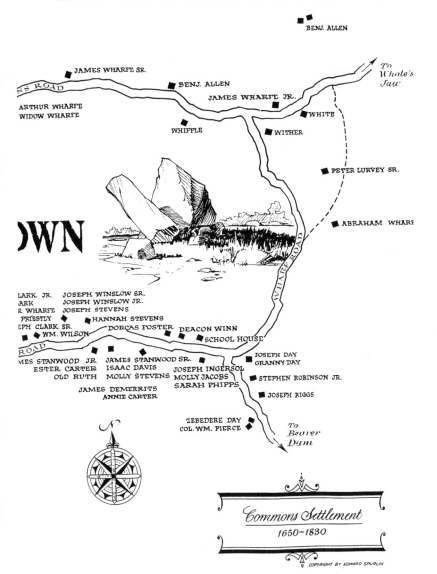

BENJ. ALLEN

JAMES WHARFE SR.

BENJ. ALLEN

JAMES WHARFE JR.

To
Whale's
Jaw

ARTHUR WHARFE
WIDOW WHARFE

WHITE

WHIPPLE

WITHER

PETER LURVEY SR.

ABRAHAM WHARF

OWN

LARK JR.   JOSEPH WINSLOW SR.
ARK   JOSEPH WINSLOW JR.
R WHARFE   JOSEPH STEVENS
PRIESTLY   HANNAH STEVENS
EPH CLARK SR.   DORCAS FOSTER   DEACON WINN
WM. WILSON   SCHOOL HOUSE
ROAD

MES STANWOOD JR.   JAMES STANWOOD SR.
ESTER CARTER   ISAAC DAVIS   JOSEPH INGERSOL
OLD RUTH   MOLLY STEVENS   MOLLY JACOBS
SARAH PHIPPS

JOSEPH DAY
GRANNY DAY

STEPHEN ROBINSON JR.

JOSEPH RIGGS

JAMES DEMERRITS
ANNIE CARTER

ZEBEDERE DAY
COL. WM. PIERCE

To
Beaver
Dam

N

Commons Settlement
1650~1830

COPYRIGHT BY EDWARD SPURLIN

to help Dorcas boost over the iron cooking pot she carried.

Dorcas lifted her dress over her thin legs and bounded over the rocks as lightly as a squirrel. Once over the wall, the two were on their way again. In the half light, small houses built of logs chinked with stone and clay began to appear. Most were not much larger than some of the boulders scattered ahead of them, and a few were already crumbling to disrepair. Cattle, too, made their way through the spread of boulders. The dim shapes munched at the meager fodder of the Common, as oblivious as Dorcas and Josiah of the panoramic view of Ipswich and Sandy Bays, or of the familiar wherries dimly visible along the shore. The common land they walked on was worth little or nothing, and was available to all for the taking.

"Your great-great grandfather, Bartholomew, owned six acres given to him by the courts for pasturage," Josiah told Dorcas. "We might as well use it for our house."

"Why did God leave all those rocks on the Common, Father?"

"Guess he stopped right here with his burden. 'This is the best place on my earth,'" he said. Josiah adjusted his own burden and grinned at her. "The best place for Dorcas Foster, at any rate, he added under his breath.

"No Britisher will ever find the Common. I'll see to that!"

Josiah was too young himself not to feel the excitement from the meeting the previous night. He was angry at the British, angry at the coercive taxes they proposed that fishermen had no way of paying, even if they had wanted to pay them, and he was eager to be off to Boston to settle the matter.

By the time Josiah had bent over the table to sign his name the night before, one side of the paper had been filled with scrawled signatures. His eye scanned the list as he wrote. They were young men, these signers, most of them not over twenty years old. He recognized the names of few older men, hugging thirty like himself. He had scratched his name and handed the pen on to another. In spite of the excitement in his chest, he felt nearer forty as he made his way home, with the care of his small daughter on his mind.

Dorcas had made their breakfast gruel by the light of one candle, while Josiah gathered their possessions, and they were on their way to the Common before daylight.

For weeks, Josiah had been laying his plans and building the house for Dorcas. As he made his rounds in his wherry (a small boat used for inshore fishing), he had known that he must leave Dorcas; that he must plan for her safety. British ships sailed closer to shore each day. The *Falcon* incident the week before, when British crewmen had tried to come ashore to steal some sheep, had set off new fears for the safety of those who lived near the harbor.

"Did the British go to the meeting last night, Father?" Josiah chuckled at her ignorance, glad she was too young to understand the danger that threatened them.

"Oh, no, the Red Coats will never tie up at Gloucester Harbor, we'll see to that," he assured her. "And they'll never find our house here on the Common."

Their house had no door and Josiah entered first to set down the weight he carried. The one room was tiny and bare of furniture, with only a rough fireplace of stone and clay for cooking and warmth.

Dorcas set down the cooking pot she carried and began to remove from it the wooden spoons, two wooden bowls and two pewter cups, all the utensils she would need or, for that matter, all they owned. Next to the pot on the dirt floor she set a rag of gingham, tied like a sack, that held all the treasures of a small girl's heart: the acorn dolls with the stick arms and legs, and the acorn table and stool for the make-believe doll house.

Josiah wasted no time. Daylight had barely filtered inside the house when he untied from around his neck the sleeves of a shirt that made the lumpy bundle on his chest, and held all the clothes they owned. On the floor, beside the bundle, he placed his rifle, the pair of oars, and a wooden bucket that served alternately as a bait bucket and as an oil bucket for the cod livers.

On a wooden peg he hung his new guernsey jacket (made of coarse wool and cotton twill brought from England). Then he lost no time in setting about to build a bed of boughs on a poplar frame, similar to the frames fashioned by the fishermen for drying the fish.

"Somehow, I'll have to find you a coat before cold weather comes, and William Carter has promised to make a door for your house." Josiah bent over the green boughs, tying them together for the bough bed. "More boughs," he told her. "Come on."

Dorcas followed her father through the door opening, scurrying about the pastureland to gather the low creeping juniper vines that wound around the blueberry bushes and clung to the boulders, theirs for the taking.

As they returned with their arms filled, Easter Carter peered from her doorway. "Have never a fear for the child, Josiah," she called out. "William and I will keep a weather eye out for her, and I'll sleep with her nights."

Josiah nodded his thanks and went on with his preparations. By the time he had finished making the bough bed, and had satisfied himself that Dorcas would be safe and well cared for, small fishing wherries were already scattered over the bay, making their morning rounds. Only then did he take time for a hasty glance that told him many boats were missing from the bay; that other fishermen were preparing to leave as he was. His gaze shifted to the tidy pile of wood stacked for the fireplace. Dorcas had helped him gather it one day after lending a hand to build the fireplace. She had gathered small stones from among the boulders, and, after her father had cut the saplings for the framework of the house, she had helped him carry them from the nearby cutting area.

One of the corner posts was a spar from some wrecked vessel. Dorcas had spotted it at the harbor, and Josiah had carried it all the way to the Common. Good old Parson Winslow and Easter Carter had come to admire its sturdiness and to speculate on the wreck it had come from. Every bit of flotsam had its story to tell and it was fitting that this one should begin its new story for the seaman, Josiah Foster, and for his daughter, whose every ancestor had spent his life at sea.

"That spar thinks it's still holding up a sail." There was pride in Josiah's voice as he stroked the corner post. To him every detail of a vessel was alive, indeed was his life, until talk of the stamp tax reached Gloucester harbor. Until then, there was little talk of anything but fish, but all thought of fishing vanished when he signed up as crewman on a vessel to drive the British off with their tax plan. He was eager to be off.

Josiah had planned well for Dorcas. On the shelf, by the fireplace, were some slabs of dried cod fish, a jug of molasses, and a scoop for the buckets of flour and cornmeal. The vegetable garden that he had planted to provide her with most of the food she would need through the summer, already showed green shoots. He stepped through the door opening. On one side, his leg brushed his bait bucket, and on the opposite side of the doorway stood his well-worn killick, the smooth stone he had used all his life for an anchor. He kicked the stone in a gentle farewell as he turned to Dorcas. "This killick brings good luck. See you take care of it."

Josiah nodded and waved to Easter Carter, then he was off down the footpath they had traveled in the early morning mist. He turned and waved once more. "Wait for me," he called out. "I'll be back soon."

Josiah was probably one of the 375 Cape Ann men who perished either at sea, in battle, or in prison, and, if his worn down killick brought any good luck to his daughter, it was rarely evident throughout her lifetime. She lived her seventy-five years awaiting her father's return, and though she waited in vain, she had time for neither tears nor fears.

In July, the blueberries ripened and she could fill her

father's bait bucket in no time without losing sight of her open front door. When the green foliage of summer turned into a brilliant palette of autumn colors, she picked the tiny grey bayberries with their delicate wild fragrance of the Commons woodland. After the bay-berries, on a sunny day in November, she gathered the scarlet barberries (called shoe pegs), removed their stems, and cooked up a tasty sauce sweetened with molasses.

All this Dorcas learned from Easter Carter. From Easter, too, she learned how to preserve the blueberries and barberries for her winter food, and how to make candles from the bayberries, not only to brighten the shadowy corners of her cabin, but also to trade for staples at the harbor.

When spring came to the Common she tramped through the southern woods of Sandy Bay to pick the aromatic laurel, or through Joppa to the shore where, at low tide, she could wade to Salt Island to pick dogtooth violets, lilies of the valley, and the golden Dutchman's breeches. On her way home she passed houses of fisher-men who gave her fish to carry back over the gravel path to the Common.

Eventually, forty houses had emerged on the Com-mon, along with the house Josiah had built for Dorcas. One of the houses contained a family with seventeen children, including three sets of twins, so Dorcas never had to be alone. She spent a part of many days helping with the care of babies and sick neighbors.

By the time Dorcas had become a young woman, danger from the British,as well as from the Barbary pirates, had all but vanished from Cape Ann. After the Falcon incident, when all attempts of British crewmen to supplement their fish diets by stealth had been fore-stalled by Gloucster men, no further effort was made to actually invade Cape Ann until the War of 1812. (At which time, British seamen succeeded in capturing some vessels at one of the wharves and holding them for $200 ransom.)

After the wars, fishing and shipping gradually re-turned to Cape Ann, and many families living at the Common then returned to the harbor, for it was the coves and the harbors, after all, that were the sensitive fingertips of all Cape Ann. Only those who could afford nothing better remained in the houses at the Common, mostly widows who had no choice but to stay in their out of the way homes.

A certain prosperity, however, had returned to the harbor. In a short time, the more prosperous began to jeer and laugh at their former neighbors, the poor widows of the Common, who now had only dogs as com-panions and protectors. These thoughtless ones, now disdainful of their old way of life, nevertheless returned now and then to pick blueberries, even as they taunted and ridiculed as "witches" the widows in their tattered clothes, and scorned the area as "Dogtown Common."

Dorcas Foster was one of those who had little choice but to spend her entire life at Dogtown Common. She married at age twenty-two, the first of three marriages, and bore three children within the decade. Her first two husbands met the fate of so many Cape Ann fishermen; both were lost on fishing trips to the Grand Banks.

At the time the sea claimed her first husband, Dorcas, surrounded as she was by the old mysteries of the Common and the superstitions of the sea, had a premonition of disaster. Although word had reached her that her husband's ship had been sighted on the way home, it never arrived in Gloucester harbor. One morning, Dorcas arose at dawn to scan the horizon as usual, and, as she looked off over Ipswich Bay, she clearly saw his ship. In moments, she saw her husband coming up the footpath in the distance. He was carrying a small bundle of personal effects. She hastened to start a fire in the fireplace and to prepare his breakfast, but her husband failed to appear at the doorway. She went outside again and searched about the boulders in vain. Later that morning, the captain of another vessel came to bring the sad news that her husband had been lost at sea.

Following Cape Ann's custom, Dorcas married again, a widower with two sons, and a third son was soon added to the family. This made six children for Dorcas to care for in the tiny house her father had built for her. In a short time, however, she had not only lost a second husband to the sea, but also her two stepsons. The two young men, with three companions, strolled about the wharf at Gloucester harbor, although a strict Sunday law forbade activity of this kind. Catching sight of the feared tything man, a constable hired to round up recalcitrants, the five young men jumped into a small boat tied up at the wharf. The boat overturned with the weight of the five and they all drowned in the harbor.

Grief of the sea, terrors of war, and poverty pursued Dorcas throughout her life. By the time she was thirty-two years old she had married her third husband, Joseph Smith, a ship's captain during the War of 1812, and had two more children. But the sea held still more grief for her. Eventually, two of her children by her first husband were lost at sea. The total of her losses was two husbands, two children, and two step-children, but Dorcas Foster was only a part of the story of Dogtown Common.

12

The Witches of Dogtown

EASTER CARTER WAS A NEAR NEIGHBOR, TEACHER, AND friend for Dorcas Foster. Easter was a young woman in her mid-thirties who lived with her brother, William. Their father had brought them to Cape Ann from England, and their quiet, dignified bearing earned them the respect of their neighbors. The Carter house, the only two-story house on the Common, was constructed of clapboards fastened together with wooden pegs. Easter was popular with the young people because she told their fortunes, and her house became the social center of Dogtown Common. The young men and women came early, and often spent the entire day while Easter foretold their future loves. Meanwhile, they ate from the pot of boiled cabbage, and munched on johnny cake that Easter cooked for them.

When the teenagers searched for a way to repay her, they came up with a unique idea. Each of them brought whatever scraps of wallpaper they could find, and one day they papered the entire house, every room from floor to ceiling, until it resembled a patchwork quilt, as colorful as Becky's barbershop at the harbor.

As popular as Easter was, however, competition challenged her skills at fortune telling, for spinning fortunes became the neighborhood pastime. Becky Rich was considered the best fortune teller on Dogtown Common. Becky examined coffee grounds more often than palms to foretell the future, and, when Easter, in her old age, moved to the harbor, Becky Rich moved into Easter's house, where many young people still flocked for insights into their current love affairs.

One advantage for Becky was the location of her house, for the old house that had once belonged to Easter Carter was the first structure along the pasture path. Across the path lived the Day family with their seventeen children. By the time Easter had moved to the harbor, and Becky had taken over the practice of telling fortunes, a small grocery store had been built, as well as a blacksmith shop and a schoolhouse. Becky never lacked for an audience for her forecasts of the future.

Others tried their skills at fortune telling, along with Easter Carter and Becky Rich. Some went so far as to mix a "witch's brew" of potent herbs to concoct a potion of greater power. Herbs had always been used for medicinal purposes and a careless housekeeper, who neglected her herb garden, was said to "turn comfort out the door." The tops of the "weeds" were cut off when "thick as raindrops," but gathered in dry weather, "while in full flower, before Dog Days!" They were then dried in the shade and saved for the next emergency.

Early Cape Anners also gathered marsh hay, meadow grass, meadow mud, and sea weed, all useful and free-for-the-taking fertilizers. In addition, they possessed a "magic power to dispel odors." At the same time, the Cape Ann code of health prohibited the use of tobacco for any purpose except to kill insects.

Moll Jacobs was another fortune teller. She taught "the art" to her daughter, Rachel, and to "Old Ruth" one of many black men who came to Cape Ann by way of trading vessels. Moll acquired the most shameful of all reputations, for rumors spread that she sheltered strangers, and once she had been accused of maintaining a house of ill-fame.

Tammy Younger, too, was well known as a fortune telling "witch," and eventually it was Tammy who became the acknowledged "Queen" of the witches of Dogtown Common. "Tammy" was a nickname for Thomasine, born at Cape Ann July 28, 1753. Her parents,

William and Lucy, were married by the Reverend John White, the first pastor of the first church on Cape Ann.

A single poplar tree shaded the house where the Younger family lived, a house so well built that it remained on its stone foundation into the nineteenth century. The house sat nearer to the harbor than many of the other houses, and Tammy, though barely more than a teenager, had the advantage of a good teacher. At the harbor, rumors floated about in whispers that Tammy had even inherited witchery skills from her aunt, Lucy George. When Dorcas Foster came to live at the Common, Tammy was twenty-three years old, and already she was highly respected, though feared, for her exceptional powers to conjure up magic and mystery.

Tammy's aunt Lucy, it was claimed, had been so gifted with witch powers that she had only to stand in the doorway to "bewitch" grazing cattle and obtain her quota of milk. Her niece, Tammy, was said to have inherited all these powers and more. At times, their neighbors asserted, Tammy and her friend, Peg Wesson, combined their talents. If in need of fuel, they bewitched a load of wood from a passing wagon. If hungry, they used the same "magic" to obtain fish at the wharf; and, if they felt vindictive, as they often did, they pooled their powers to prevent a neighbor's bread from rising. Stories were told that the girls went so far as to cause the hair to fall out of the head of an unsuspecting victim.

Tammy was not the tall, jut-jawed witch of fiction. On the contrary, she was short of stature, and her plump figure attested that she somehow found enough to eat, whether by magic or otherwise.

As Tammy grew older, eventually living alone as did many of the women of Dogtown Common, stories naturally circulated about her extraordinary powers. Some who lived at the harbor accused her with disdain, of smoking snuff. Others charged that she permitted "lawless" men to stay at her house; that she associated with card players, fortune tellers, and even pirates. If she asked for help for so much as to carry a pail of water, no one dared to refuse her for one and all feared her mysterious powers.

In time, foot travelers stole by her house with only furtive glances, scarcely daring to pass, while Tammy, they claimed, peered out from a tiny window hidden behind the underbrush. From this window, which Tammy opened and shut at will by a length of rope, she was said to cast a hex on anyone who crossed her will.

When Tammy died in 1829 at the age of seventy-six, even more stories began to circulate about a cache of money and a snuff box found in her cellar, as well as her effective skills with "magic."

True or not, Tammy's "magic" was buried with her in a hand-made wooden coffin, and many who knew her asserted that her wicked reputation was undeserved. Some of her friends even assured the critics that she had been mistaken for her aunt, Lucy George. In any case, in deference to Tammy's reputation as a "Queen," she was accorded the finest funeral available in Dogtown Common.

In her last years, Tammy had become a great care to her nephew, Oliver, who complained to a neighbor of his aunt's dependence on him, and of the enormous financial responsibility he bore for her property at the Common.

"Why, Oliver," the neighbor said in surprise, "that is your own property. Your father willed it to you."

Oliver looked at the neighbor in doubtful astonishment. "Are you sure? How do you know this?"

The neighbor nodded. "I know for sure, for I signed the will as a witness."

Still incredulous, Oliver waited until the next day when his aging aunt had left the house to visit a neighbor. Then he entered and searched the house until he found the property deed tucked away in the back of a drawer. With positive proof that the property was to be his eventually, Oliver was more than willing to give his Aunt Tammy the proper care as long as she lived. For the funeral arrangements when she died, however, he sought the advice of old Mrs. Pulsifer, who had attended Tammy in her final illness.

"Have John Hodgkins, the cabinet maker, make the finest coffin that can be made," Mrs. Pulsifer directed, "and have him mark her name on a silver name plate!"

Oliver followed Mrs. Pulsifer's instructions, and, in addition, he ordered that "cordials, wines, and the best beverages" be served after the ceremony, although it was customary to serve only the more commonplace rum at Cape Ann funerals.

On the day before the funeral, John Hodgkins worked all day to finish Tammy's coffin, but the day was dark and rainy, and night closed in before he could apply the final polish that such a splendid coffin deserved.

The weary cabinet maker stood the unfinished box in a corner of the kitchen until evening when he resumed his work by candle light. With a wad of beeswax he rubbed down the soft pine, and polished the wood to a burnished gold worthy of Tammy's trip to eternity. While he worked, the rain increased in fury, and John Hodgkins knew he must not return his creation to his outside workshop and expose the freshly polished pine to the rain. Once more he stood the coffin in a corner of the kitchen to dry until morning.

When the Hodgkins children made their way to bed that night, through the kitchen and to the attic stairway, their single candle cast eerie shadows about Tammy's gleaming coffin.

"We'll not sleep with Tammy's coffin in the kitchen," they screamed.

Their mother, at first impatient with the children's fears, took one look at the coffin in the corner of her kitchen, and she, too, raised her voice in protest.

"Get that thing out of my kitchen! I shan't sleep a wink, any more than the children!"

"But the rain will spot the finish," objected the meticulous cabinet maker.

"Spot the finish or not," his wife argued, "I'll not stay in this house with Tammy's coffin!"

John had little choice but to struggle through the rain dragging Tammy's coffin, but the following morning, spots and all, Oliver, Mrs. Pulsifer, and the neighbors buried her with all the splendor befitting her royal status.

Tammy's demise brought to an end the extremes of "magic power" that had gripped the minds of settlers on the Common for a century. The mysterious "voices" were at last stilled, leaving in a misty obscurity whatever role this ghostly village had been destined to play in the development of Cape Ann.

For many Cape Anners, and visitors as well, stories of the primitive conditions on Dogtown Common faded into legend. They became merely tales told by the fearful; perhaps the last remaining link with worn-out superstitions. For still others, it was one more pause, one more looking back, before moving onward.

In any case, Dogtown Common had served its purpose of providing a refuge for those who shrank from the unknown. When the danger passed, when the wars ceased, the world came crowding in to Cape Ann. The magic of the palm and the coffee grounds and the herb pot gave way, at last, to the magic of real money. Among the fish houses along the waterfront, all manner of small industries sprouted; industries that fulfilled the needs of the fishermen; industries that called the young stragglers back to the harbor.

For one hundred years, Dogtown Common had soothed the frightened and fed the hungry, but eventually a Cape Ann economist, Roger Babson, descendant of Isabel, perceived yet another character role for Dogtown Common to play in the future of Cape Ann.

"This primitive village," he said, "taught us a valuable lesson in economics. This settlement of no more than forty houses, is a microcosm, the exact pattern that all families, cities, and countries live through. In such a pattern," he explained, "we find four stages, whether family, city, or country. First, the improvement of an area for living. Then follows comparative comfort and prosperity, and after this there is a gradual decline. In the end comes a depression and downfall."

It was time for Dogtown Common to die, along with Tammy Younger, and for other pieces of the Cape Ann pattern to fall into place. Still, economist Babson, with all the vision of John Smith, foresaw a way to perpetuate Dogtown Common for future tourists.

During the Depression of the 1930s, Babson engaged John Talvitie and other stone cutters of Finnish descent, to carve miniature sermons on the boulders of the Common. Under the direction of these skilled craftsmen, entirely by hand tools carried over the ancient footpath, the superb workmanship of the project proceeded. In time, letters ten inches high spelled out words of wisdom on the ageless rocks. Such moral teachings as Get a Job; Keep out of Debt; Never Try, Never Win, will endlessly counsel the wanderer of Dogtown Common.

This guidance, however, came to the Common long after the last tenant had vacated and the last house left to crumble into ruin.

Tammy Younger and the other "witches" were gone. The wars had taken their toll of fishermen and boats. About half the population had turned to farming,

though neither fishing nor farming brought more than the basic necessities for survival in the bleak Cape Ann climate. The Cape's standard of living had risen only slightly since its earliest days. The fishing industry at Gloucester, nevertheless, was growing imperceptibly, and, just as sizes and styles of boats were changing, just as the sea changes incessantly, so Cape Ann's way of life had begun to change, as well.

13

New Industries for Cape Ann

THE GROWING FISHING INDUSTRY AT GLOUCESTER HAR-
bor called for special needs. The old-fashioned stone
killick of Josiah Foster's day no longer sufficed, and the
fishermen needed stronger anchors for the larger boats.
Also, they required waterproof clothing, spars for their
new vessels, fishing tackle, fog horns, nets and twine,
sails, and copper paint. Hake was still being caught in
the quantities of John Smith's time, and someone discovered that sheets of a gelatin-like substance could be
made from the hake "sounds," an air bladder inside the
fish, near the backbone.

There was an instant market for this new product,
called isinglass, which was found to be useful to clarify
and settle beer. To make the most of this discovery,
carpenters were hired to build a specially designed fish

house on Bearskin Neck, Rockport; the first fishhouse to be built two stories high! Competition soon expanded this new industry so that eventually a larger structure was built near the railroad station. Barbara Malone Buckley recalled watching the process as a small child, while her grandfather managed the business. "The hake sounds were soaked in huge square vats," she related, "then ground to a gelatin mush and crushed between wooden rollers (later metal rollers) into thin strips." She then followed the strips as they were carried upstairs, where women stretched them out to dry. Her adventure was complete when her grandfather permitted her to blow the noon whistle for the workers' lunch time. The finished product sold well, until Prohibition put an end to the industry. Its last customer was Narragansett Breweries.

Women, as always, adapted their skills to meet new demands. They initiated their own home industries, and one of the most important accomplishments, but now almost forgotten, was the knitting of nippers for the fishermen.

The handmade nippers, an urgent need of the fishing industry and always in demand, were bands of coarse wool yarn, knitted thick, in the shape of a doughnut, with a groove in the middle deep enough to hold the fishing lines and protect the fisherman's hands at

A hake sound

the same time. These nippers were designed especially to meet the needs of the trawlers and handliners.

The demand for knit nippers was so great that ship outfitters bought them from the women at fifty cents a pair. One crewman usually required from four to six pairs, depending on the length of his trip at sea. On long trips of three or four months, the skipper bought an extra supply of nippers to dole out to his crew.

Women soon learned that they could knit these nippers and sell them to augment their church treasuries. This became a favorite way of earning funds for church needs, as well as satisfying needs of the fishermen. In a period of two hundred years, nippers were sold in the millions, many to Canadian markets, before handlining and trawling went out of style and the demand for them declined.

In 1879, the women of a Gloucester church knitted nippers one evening each week, and at the same time determined to "improve their minds and suppress vain conversation." While they worked, they took turns reading from a book titled *Nevins Practical Thoughts*. In twelve months time the women improved their minds and knitted nippers that brought $150 into their church treasury.

Yet, as enterprising as Cape Anners were in their new industries, fulfilling the needs of the fishermen, selling nippers, herbs, and blueberries, no one had so much as guessed at a use for their great gift of granite.

14

The Gift of Granite

THE OCEAN THUNDERED ON, ALWAYS SPECTACULAR AND noisy, as if to call attention to the rock formations it had carved. More decades must pass, however, before anyone could imagine what to do with all that stone which, in fact, contained a secret almost as miraculous as the gift of granite itself. The secret, locked so snug, soundless, and invisible inside the granite, must wait, as in fairy tales of old, for a key to fit the lock.

At last, a Cape Ann man, Nehemiah Knowlton, a resourceful man and one for whom fishing held no charms, took the first step toward unlocking the secret. He learned, through trial and error, how to split a piece of granite that could be used for a mooring stone. With this achievement, Nehemiah's mind pushed on to

A granite quarry.

dreams even more fantastic; he placed an advertise-
ment in a Boston newspaper, and began to sell pieces of
Cape Ann rock for a living. This enterprising man,
unaware that he, like John Smith, had been singled out
to lead Cape Ann through another step of transition,
cut 300 tons of stone from a landscape that barely
missed it.

Meanwhile, as Nehemiah took rock from ocean
sculpture to the craft of man, he formed several part-
nerships with other men to help fill the orders that
deluged him. The growing city of Boston asked for
granite blocks to pave its muddy streets, and to build
the Customs House. Word spread and carried the name
of Cape Ann to distant cities—New Orleans, Wash-

Stone Bridge.

ington, New York. Statues, naval drydocks, and light-houses emerged from Cape Ann rocks.

The gift of granite brought a prosperity that Cape Ann had never known; such prosperity that the villagers could, at last, afford to use the rocks themselves. Not only did they build foundations for their houses that would last forever, they cut massive blocks to use for door steps, door sills, fence posts, and hitching posts for their horses. They cut flat blocks as mooring stones for their boats, and they built great wharves of stone to withstand centuries of ocean storms. Some blocks they polished for everlasting memorials to loved ones.

Customers spoke of the stone cutters' handiwork as "granite of character," applying the words "hard as granite" to both men and material. A few learned a special skill; that of pinpointing the grain or "rift" of the granite to be cut, and this became a matter of pride as well as an art. This special skill was tedious with their simple tools, and the pay was as paltry as fishermens' pay. Still, 500 men, including some fishermen, eventually worked the granite quarries.

Ironically, the industry of such "lasting" quality failed to last forever. Whereas, at one time nearly 500 men had worked the quarries; in the end, about all searching eyes could see were derricks rising skyward from the stone chips, and unsightly scars on the ledges.

Nevertheless, the giver of the gift, the force that brought all the rocks there in the first place, had no intention of giving up so easily. Undergrowth appeared to cover the scars on the landscape. Bare walls of rock mellowed with age, and tourists, with the eye of an artist, found new beauty in the dark and lustrous tones of red and green and brown.

More and more artists came to study the rock in all the varied colors and shapes, and in a short time, scarcely noticed, yet another change began to unfold. From the art of the stone cutter emerged the art of the painter, who transferred to canvas the shadows and hues of the granite. Then, even with millions of tons of granite cut away, the amazing gift could be admired and treasured for generations to come.

Close by the old quarries, Nehemiah's dream had come true. His descendants eventually built a wharf and a breakwater overlooking Sandy Bay harbor, the same harbor where once stone sloops slipped lines from that first mooring stone and sailed to distant ports, carrying tons of the precious stone.

Just as Nehemiah fulfilled his own dreams, perhaps in some future age someone will discover the secret locked in the stone. The secret, so satisfying to the ear of the stone cutter, was the murmuring sigh that escaped when the hand of the artisan cut to perfection a block of granite. With an ear as keenly attuned to the stone as the sense of fishermen to a brewing storm, the stone cutter unlocked the secret that lay hidden for so many centuries in the heart of the stone.

At last, out of the great gifts of stone and ocean in John Smith's Paradise, Cape Ann had advanced to an idealism of her own. From the sensitive eyes and ears of the fishermen, to the artistry of the stone worker; from the curious blend of land and sea "magic," Cape Ann moved onward in hesitant steps toward its future.

In this new direction, however, things did not always go well.

15

An Occasional Artist

THOUGH THE "STRANGE AND AWFUL STIRRINGS" WENT ON in the restless heart of the sea, at times the design and purpose of Cape Ann seemed as well hidden as the whispered sigh in the granite. The transition steps, often slow of pace as the melting of the ice centuries before, sometimes came to a standstill, and one reason for this foot dragging soon became apparent. The seafarers and stone cutters both looked with skepticism on the newcomer, the artist, who came to them with a perception even more acute and sensitive than their native Cape Anners.

Welcome or not, to Cape Ann the artists came, and from the wind and waves and rock so familiar to the fishermen and stone cutters, the artists studied design and color and form.

Although for centuries beauty had been scorned as sinful, the time had come for the people of Cape Ann, as elsewhere after the Civil War, to look for a new meaning in their lives. Ship's captains from Gloucester harbor had sailed to far away ports in the Orient. They had brought back exotic plants that were far more than the ordinary dooryard variety of old-fashioned flower beds. The gardens these ship captains planted must do justice to the larger houses they could now afford. In Gloucester, they built magnificent terraces, lawns, stone walls, hedges, summer houses, stone steps framed with plantings. In addition, they planted acres of fruit trees: plums, peaches, quinces, grapes, apples, cherries, pears, and they surrounded these with shrubs of gooseberries and raspberries. One man measured off his garden to 100 by 300 feet, and then he added statues of marble and ship's figureheads of polished wood.

Though Cape Anners had always known more grief than beauty; more fog than sunshine; more work than play; and, though most had adhered to their stern beliefs in hard work with few luxuries, they now learned how to accept a certain elegance that they had never imagined for themselves. At the same time, they soon learned to accept the newcomers in ever increasing numbers. For not only the gardens, but the quarries within, and the sea around Cape Ann, attracted

Gilbert Tucker Margeson, Rockport's first resident artist.

travelers one by one, then by the dozens, then by the hundreds.

Some came by the age-old ocean highway. Others traveled the ancient footpath of the Indians over the cut, then meandered along the shore and through the woods, now made passable for wheeled vehicles. Even more arrived by the railroad, for trains long talked about as a third route, had become a reality that at last linked Cape Ann to Boston and the world beyond.

From that other world, the world so far removed from the fishing and stone cutting, came more artists. They were transients, however, who came to study and absorb the colors and form of rocks and sea, and then return to the city. Years elapsed before one artist came to stay.

Gilbert Tucker Margeson was the first artist to choose Cape Ann for his permanent home, and, though he came more than two hundred years after the first fisherman, he was a pioneer like John Smith, Richard Tarr, John Pool, Harlakenden Symonds, and Nehemiah Knowlton; there to shape the changing pattern of Cape Ann.

Artist Margeson traveled by train to Cape Ann in 1873, and got off the train at the end of the line—Rockport. He was twenty-one years old and had been studying art in Boston, but he was soon to show the world that his heart was among the seafaring people from whom he had descended. He was born in a Nova Scotia village, not unlike the villages of Cape Ann that he came to love. As a boy, although stories such as *Captains Courageous* had not yet been written, he heard constant tales of the treacherous waters that stretched from his Nova Scotia home to the coves of Cape Ann.

As early as 1713, the Treaty of Utrecht had freed these Atlantic waters, and, if it did not entirely free

Gilbert Tucker Margeson studio.

them from pirate dangers, it at least gave political freedom for colonial fishing and commerce, and thus made safe the area from Nova Scotia and Newfoundland all the way to Cape Ann.

A direct sea lane ran from Nova Scotia to Cape Ann, and this sea lane helped to forge the many common ties of the two countries. By the time the Utrecht treaty created safe fishing grounds for both, Cape Ann fishermen and vessels were already making regular trips to the Grand Banks off Nova Scotia, and, though this was profitable, the area was a stormy, disastrous expanse. Along with the thrills and the profits of the large catch came the grim awareness that the Nova Scotia Banks were scattered with the wrecks of Cape Ann fishing vessels.

On this sea lane, over the wrecks of so many ships, the Margeson family had sailed with their young son. To escape the restrictions of French provincialism, the family had settled in Boston. Somehow, they had found the money to hire an art teacher for their gifted son who eventually made his way to Cape Ann, along with other visiting artists.

While others came and went, however, the young Gilbert Tucker Margeson came to stay. With his ties to the sea never out of his mind, he bought a fishing shack that had been lashed by storms for one hundred and fifty years. There, near the harbor, the fragrance of his oil paints blended with the last lingering smells of the fishing gear that had been treated with tar.

From a window in the shack, or later from an adjacent studio built of native granite, he observed with the curiosity of a student, the twice daily change of tides and the constant activity of the bright-sailed fishing boats.

A man of small build, he yet possessed a courtesy and a quiet dignity that gave him stature. With his eyes searching far beyond the busy harbor, toward the open sea, he recalled with pride his ancestor, Edmund Margeson, who had sailed from England, signed the Mayflower

Compact, and established an earlier colony at Plymouth, on the same Massachusetts coast. Or perhaps his gaze swept northward to Nova Scotia, where more Margesons had settled, and where he had spent his boyhood.

The thread of his preference for the sea had been so tightly woven that he felt impelled to preserve on canvas those subjects nearest to his heart; the ships and surf, the rocky coastline, the fog and storms.

In those days, like his fishermen neighbors, Gilbert Tucker Margeson owned scarcely a chair to furnish his seaside studio. But then, there was not only little time to paint, there was no income from his efforts. He was a part-time painter by necessity, perhaps Cape Ann's first "moonlighter," for he shared his hours of painting with long hours of work at his stationery store where he sold "pens, inks, periodicals" and artists' supplies.

Meanwhile, this young man with the soul of an artist, yearning to impart to others the wonders he saw in Cape Ann, found still another way to strengthen the link between Cape Ann and the outer world. He began to study telegraphy, and in a short time he became one of the first on Cape Ann to send and receive messages by way of Western Union wires.

It was this new skill, in addition to his ability as an artist, that brought about his friendship with Alexander

Graham Bell. For Bell, too, had begun to study electricity in telegraphy and to lecture in Boston about the new phenomenon. While Bell carried on his lectures in Boston, Margeson began to work in the telegraph office, not only to earn a living but also because this developing method of communication had been of great interest to his family in Nova Scotia. At that time, there was already talk of plans to lay an Atlantic cable from Europe to Halifax, and it was natural for the young Margeson to combine this interest with his art.

Each day, after his day's work in his store and later at the telegraph office, Margeson stood, with brush in hand, before his easel adding final strokes to yet another painting, sometimes offering brief lessons to an eager observer.

"You see," he would say, pointing to his canvas, "A ship is proud. I always paint a ship with its prow up, never down into the waves. Remember, a ship is proud."

From the sea came the lessons of the artist in the same way they had emerged long before for the fishermen, and in the sea around Cape Ann, Alexander Graham Bell was to follow and search for answers.

16

One Artist Comes to Stay

WHILE GILBERT TUCKER MARGESON CONTINUED HIS WORK at his easel, in his shop, and with telegraphy, Bell's studies led him nearer and nearer to Cape Ann, where he and Margeson were destined to meet. Bell, born in Edinburgh, Scotland in 1847, headed for Boston at age 26. Margeson, born in Black Rock, Nova Scotia, and five years younger than Bell, came to Boston at an earlier age but there they missed each other by a few months, for Margeson left Boston the year Bell arrived there.

Nevertheless, their common interests eventually were to bring them together. While Margeson's parents provided lessons in visual art for their young son in Boston, Bell's parents had provided their son with an acute and highly trained ear for sound. His father was an experimenter in sounds and his mother was a musician and artist of ability.

From his father's studies in Visible Speech, Bell went on to study pitches and resonance of vowel sounds, and it was in pursuit of sounds that Bell went to Boston to study and lecture on his experiments. Then, he carried his experiments with deaf children, including Helen Keller and a five-year-old boy, to nearby Salem. From Salem, it was but a few miles to Cape Ann-side, that area of shoreline north of Boston nicknamed by the early fishermen. And so, one summer, Bell went to Cape Ann for a vacation of work and study.

In the room he rented in the basement of Andrew Mason's drug store at Pigeon Cove, he set up a few gadgets simply fashioned: some batteries, electro-magnets, a few tuning forks. Then he ran a single experimental wire from the drug store to Story's General Store, a distance of a few hundred feet. Already, he realized he could converse with a friend down the street without leaving his house. He worked all that summer to perfect his telephone in order to submit it for a patent. Many years after Bell's telephone became a world-changing invention, one of his biographers wrote, "The wonder of Bell's creation lies in its simplicity."

The simplicity of Cape Ann attracted Bell, and he chose the simple pleasures that Cape Ann had to offer for his brief moments of relaxation. For these quiet reflections he hired young Jim Griffin to row him about the harbor.

When the slim, dark-haired student-inventor, wearing side whiskers, leaned back in the stern of the lobster dory, his sensitive ears were attuned to every sound; those same sounds the Cape Ann fishermen had known so well, in the same harbor that once echoed the commands of Barbary pirates. He heard the waves splashing against the sides of the dory with a persistence akin to his own. He heard the blunted thrust of the oars against the thole pins, and he heard, too, the ancient urgency of the tides and the subdued song of the wind.

Bell's trained and brilliant mind asked questions of the ocean textbook in the same way the early fishermen had sought answers. But Bell dreamed of new ways to convey sounds to others far beyond Cape Ann. He dreamed of spanning uncharted space with sound, and he imagined that currents of air over Sandy Bay could carry all these sounds to the eardrum. Sometimes he tested his dream on young Jim Griffin in the dory.

"Say, Jim. Do you want to get rich?"

The younger boy could only nod as a grin spread over his tanned face.

"Then buy stock in my telephone," he urged. "Twenty-five cents a share."

Jim had no coins to jingle in his pocket, except what few Bell paid him to row him about the harbor.

Bell went on with his experiments, working at night like a conspirator. He was already aware that he had made a discovery of great significance to the world. Meanwhile, the mutual interest in telegraphy brought Bell and Margeson together, and they became friends, although their separate efforts at communication for Cape Ann were uniquely different.

Margeson went to work for Western Union, which meant his ties to Bell came to an abrupt end after Bell received a patent for his telephone. In March 1876 he offered to sell the patent to Western Union for $100,000, but Western Union was satisfied at the time with its own devices for transmitting sixty words per minute, and the president of Western Union rejected the offer.

Bell returned to his lectures at Boston University, and Margeson painted his great sea pictures for pleasure and sent telegraph messages for a living. While they worked, yet a third effort was under way at reinforcing Cape Ann's mooring lines to the outer world.

17

Ties to the World Beyond

THE NEW VENTURE THAT WAS ABOUT TO UNFOLD QUICKLY captivated the artistic minds of both Bell and Margeson, for this idea, too, embraced the mysteries of communication. They both followed the plans with whole-hearted enthusiasm, for they began close by, in Rockport.

Along that part of the shoreline that lay between the harbors of Gloucester and Rockport, where hopeful and adventurous visitors had never stopped searching for pots of pirate gold, stretched a beach strewn with more pebbles than sand, and appropriately named Pebblestone Beach. This beach, sometimes called by its old name of Pobblestone Beach, was about to share in a world famous event—the laying of a telegraph cable across the Atlantic Ocean.

Twenty-seven years before the cable finally landed at this Cape Ann beach, it began its historic development in Ireland. The tiny Irish bays—Doulus and Foilhummurum—were as unpronounceable as Tragabigzanda and as little known around the world as Sandy Bay, but they had already captured the interest of scientists, financiers, and governments.

At the same time, Mrs. Young, as enterprising an Irish hotel keeper as any on Cape Ann, "begged to inform tourists" through the local Irish newspaper, of the "considerable additions to her house rendered necessary by the influx of visitors who were interested in the Atlantic cable." The additions she had in mind continued "on a modest scale" until the sixth cable ship set off for Cape Ann. Five previous attempts to land cables had varying degrees of success, and all found a connecting link at Newfoundland by the shortest distance to Ireland.

In Ireland, when the project had started on August 5, 1857, bands played and flags flew as the ship departed for America. The celebration was wasted, however, for when the ship was less than a third of the way across the ocean the cable broke and the disaster delayed the project for another year.

As repairs to the broken cable went on, further plans were under way for a third terminus at Waterville, another pin-point size Irish village. Here lived Mrs. Young, the hotel keeper, and Waterville became the base for the link that connected Ireland with Cape Ann. Even with additions to her house, Mrs. Young could not accommodate all the crewmen and their families, and some had to be housed in a hunting lodge.

Eventually, though, nearly two decades later, the steamship *Faraday*, a commercial vessel 365 feet long, with a crew of 200 men, and bearing all the latest scientific equipment, was on its way to Cape Ann by way of Newfoundland.

May 23, 1884, was the expected date of arrival of the Faraday (named for the most eminent scientist of the project) at Pebblestone Beach. On May 11, citizens of Rockport, anticipating this day as one of world-wide significance, held a meeting to make appropriate plans for the day's events. They planned an elaborate welcome and reception befitting the occasion, and on the planning committee was the same young man who had followed Bell's telephone experiments and who was now the local Western Union operator, thirty-two-year-old Gilbert Tucker Margeson.

As the committee's plans progressed, the Faraday steamed closer to Pebblestone Beach, until the morning of May 22 when, at the first break of dawn, an early rising fisherman sighted the *Faraday* off Thacher Island.

The guests had arrived twenty-four hours earlier than expected! By 5:00 A.M. the ship had anchored off Thacher Island, and the news had been telegraphed from the island to the Western Union office in Rockport. In a short time a volley of gun shot from the Faraday awakened sleeping Cape Ann.

Citizens of Rockport, the nearest Cape Ann village and location of Pebblestone Beach, were soon firing off their own canon, ringing church bells, and hastily setting off for Pebblestone Beach to share in the excitement. They walked or rode the two-and-a-half-mile distance in carriages or on bicycles, rowed their boats— pretty girls, exuberant boys, proud town officials, matrons carrying parasols of "shot silk," and little girls gowned in their best embroidered dresses with handmade flounces of matching colors, and worn over sateen slips.

The townspeople of Cape Ann lost none of the excitement or historical significance of the day, nor did the throngs of tourists who streamed from off the Cape all day long. They cheered wildly, and then laughingly covered their ears while canons shot off a salute of thirty-eight guns. Gloucester bands joined Rockport musicians to play "Hail Columbia" and "Rule Britannia," and the crew of the Faraday went on working.

The *Faraday*, by now at anchor a half-mile off shore,

Landing of the trans-Atlantic cable at Pebble Beach.

lost no time in making ready the coil of cable which crewmen payed out and recoiled onto three large rafts made of inflated rubber bags with a board laid on top, then onto a fourth pontoon made of boats lashed together and also covered with boards. Six hundred and ninety-two fathoms of cable were coiled on the rafts—over 4,000 feet, four-fifths of a mile!

Three boat crews of men wearing life preservers were sent ashore through tumbling surf, with all boats lashed together and towed by yet another boat. Once landed safely, men slowly uncoiled the cable over the stern of each boat, then hauled the heavy cable through a trench already dug along the water line. Then the cable was threaded through the pebbles to the newly built cable house, and there secured.

The yelling, cheering throng of onlookers followed the cable down the beach, while the small boats crowded in close, as well, to marvel at the wonder of linking their fishing village with that other world of England and Ireland, from which their forebears had come.

Meanwhile, the young artist–Western Union operator, who had helped to plan the day's celebration, slipped away from the crowd unnoticed, and hurried to his office on Bearskin Neck. His first duty was to inform the world by way of his Western Union wires.

By ten o'clock that morning the cable had been laid, and Gilbert Tucker Margeson had dispatched to the world's newspapers the front page news of the cable that was about to connect, by a dot-dash code, a tiny Cape Ann village and the rest of the world. But the work of the *Faraday* crew had yet to be completed.

To the disappointment of the townspeople, the captain courteously declined their invitation to dinner and speeches. Now that the shore end of the cable was laid, the *Faraday* must return at once to a point 250 miles at sea where they had left a cable end on a buoy. This must now be spliced and made ready for the first trans-Atlantic message. Then, without further delay, the

Faraday weighed anchor and steamed off, trailing the cable behind to make the necessary connection some 250 miles eastward.

In the evening the dinner went on as planned, with young girls in white dresses serving the tables set for eighty dignitaries, including the foremost electricians of the day, along with the planning committee and the man who had scooped the message of the cable to the world, Gilbert Tucker Margeson.

After that gala day, Cape Ann was in the public eye as never before, but still not widely known. Although the new technology, along with the gardens and the rock formations, brought an increasing number of visitors, it was not until the pleasures of bathing were discovered that each new season brought more tourists.

18

They Came to Swim

THE ROCK-LINED "GENTLEMEN'S BATH" AT HOOP POLE cove in Pigeon Cove was the last word in elegant swimming for the nineteenth century "gentlemen." Even today, the adventurous tourist can re-discover the "Bath," for the same ocean washes and refills the same natural, granite-lined swimming pool, in the same tiny cove.

To reach this cove, gentlemen guests from Pigeon Cove hotels of the 1850s strolled from the avenues to the ocean, then over slippery granite blocks that were carpeted with Iceland moss!

The moss, while providing food for sea animals, afforded also velvety soft footing for the non-swimming gentlemen.

For the energetic swimmer, nature had placed more

of Cape Ann's boulders at convenient spacing to make a solid base for divers, as well as resting places for the weary.

Furthermore, a sea breeze constantly fanned these favored gentlemen, while they inhaled "sweet, untainted air." In addition to all these pleasures for the gentlemen, the Bath at Hoop Pole Cove was "delightful, invigorating, rapturous; it caught the healing perfumes sifting from shore to inland pastures; and it was washed by daily tides of pure brine!" In short, according to one enthusiast, it was "the very ecstacy of creation!"

Alas, this secluded wonder, this healer of all ills, was denied to women. Women were permitted to bathe and swim from other rocks or coves or beaches, but never from Hoop Pole Cove. Never!

The male guests, by being so exclusive, deprived themselves of one additional pleasure. For women bathers, it was rumored, who were guests at the same hotels but banned from the "Gentlemen's Bath," were often cause for hilarious laughter. Female bathers, it seems, were of two types: one kind bathed "from a sense of duty," while the other kind bathed "for pleasure and excitement." Both types tripped daily to the bath houses, as did the men, making use of the bath houses provided for them on the rocky shore. One keen-eyed observer wrote that "the dutiful ones nerve themselves

Pebble Beach bath house, 1896.

as if going to the dentist's chair. Then they remove their hats," she wrote, "stoop down and fill the hats with water, then pour the water over head and shoulders. Following this ritual," she assured her readers, "they grip the safety rope and venture three or four plunges, then return dripping wet to the bath house."

The other kind of female swimmer, "those who love to swim," the writer went on, "plunge in with screeching and shivering, then they sit down on a wet rock and let a wave splash over them."

The Gentlemen of the Bath, unaware of the high-spirited women and the entertainment they were missing, nevertheless, sometimes let their imaginations soar as had John Smith and the early fishermen. One said he thought of himself "as a poor ship-wrecked mortal, clinging to a cold, hard rock, with great waves thundering in."

The joy of swimming added one more attraction for visitors to Cape Ann. It was no longer necessary for Cape Anners to boast about themselves. Travelers would now do the boasting for them, and as each new season brought more guests, many wondered why they had not come sooner.

19

Hotels for the Traveler

ONE OF THOSE NINETEENTH-CENTURY TOURISTS WAS
Ralph Waldo Emerson, who traveled all the way from
Concord. "I have made acquaintance with the sea," he
wrote to a friend in July 1856, after spending several
days at Pigeon Cove. "'Tis a noble, friendly power," he
continued in his letter, "and seems to say to me, 'Why
so long and slow to come?'" In the letter Emerson went
on as his friend Thoreau might have done. "Was ever
couch so magnificent? Lie down on my warm ledges and
learn that a very little hut is all you need."

Further along in the letter he wrote, "And behold the
sea—beautiful as the rose or the rainbow, full of food,
nourisher of man, and in its beauty giving a hint of that
which changes not, and is perfect!"

Of the rocks Emerson went on in his fashion, "They

Copyright 1905 by the Rotograph Co.
A 7179 Phillips Ave., Pigeon Cove, Mass.

are Romes and Ninevehs in ruin, a giant causeway, prostrate or half-piled."

The poetic words of Emerson, once set in a plaque on a rock at Andrews Point, can now be read by all tourists in the Old Castle Museum of the Sandy Bay Historical Society at Pigeon Cove.

Emerson found accommodations in one of the first hotels erected for summer guests, near the rocks he described with so much eloquence. The old hotel eventually burned but a portion of the remaining timbers was later removed to become a part of the present Ralph Waldo Emerson Inn.

Emerson was able to shape his admiration into words with more verbal skills than most tourists. As one said of him, "He made literary what most of us only feel!"

Women, however, though denied the rite of the Bath, were not to be outdone in either literary or political skills of the men.

Boat launching day at Bearskin Neck.

20

Fishermen Win One

ONE EARLY AUTHOR, ELIZABETH PHELPS, WHO WAS SUM-mering in Gloucester, wrote of the "unexpected and undreamed of delights on the other side of the Cape, at Pigeon Cove." In a later decade, yet another writer, Nathaniel Hawthorne's daughter, Hildegarde, described the Cape Ann coast as "the principal reason for owning an automobile."

As summer visitors crowded in with ever increasing numbers, the fishermen once again found it necessary to resist the newcomers, at times even to the point of defiance.

The new crisis arose over the placement of a buoy off the eastern point of Gloucester. This aid to navigation for fishermen approaching Gloucester harbor was a matter of safety to themselves, as well as to the

Fish sheds.

entire fishing industry. It was an unquestioned necessity to the fishermen. To summer visitors, however, the buoy was an intolerable disruption to the rest and relaxation they had anticipated. For this particular buoy, unlike most buoys that floated in utter silence, was a "whistling" buoy. It whistled day and night, and one after another of the annoyed visitors voiced vehement objections. These complaints forced the dispute into open controversy, while the fishermen refused to surrender.

At last, author Elizabeth Phelps, who possessed considerable political clout as it turned out, succeeded in reaching the ears of the Secretary of the Navy in Washington. The Secretary listened with sympathy to her complaint, and forthwith ordered the offending buoy removed from May to October!

This state of affairs, endangering the lives of fishermen, led to almost open warfare, but before the end of summer an unexpected romance solved the problem. The lady, Elizabeth Phelps, fell in love and married a man whose sympathies were firmly on the side of the Gloucester fishermen. As a result, the buoy was soon returned to its rightful place as an aid to navigation, while the sea and the rocks continued to share the new horizons with summer guests, with scarcely time, now, for a backward look.

21

Fish Shacks on the Necks

DESPITE THE INCREASING NUMBER OF SUMMER TOURISTS, Cape Ann fishermen went on with the business of fishing. For over two hundred years, after those first "frames and necessaries," more fish huts had emerged along the shoreline. Sometimes they were built singly, as if to stand aloof from the newcomers. At other times, though, unpainted structures rose in clusters and were simply designed to hold fishing gear and bait, or for temporary shelter while fishermen told their endless sea stories.

All around Cape Ann, narrow lengths of land separated one cove from another, probing the ocean like curious fingers. These "fingers," sometimes called "necks," were for centuries no more than strips of pasture land, as rocky and bare as Dogtown Common. They were, nevertheless, the small stages ready and waiting for the larger drama of Cape Ann.

Although the need for space—first to dry the fish, then to cut the stone, and then to build more houses and hotels for the tourists—had moved families back from the shore, it was the waterfront, with its necks and coves, that still provided the basic essentials of life— food, livelihood, and story telling.

Of all those "necks" that reached into Ipswich Bay and Sandy Bay, necks that defied storms that wracked the bayfronts in all seasons, one "neck," it now appears, was destined to stage the most remarkable of all the dramas on Cape Ann.

Bearskin Neck, less than two acres of pasture land, reached into Sandy Bay on the northeast tip of Cape Ann, challenging the Atlantic on all sides. On this rocky and bare land, the business of fishing had prevailed, with only occasionally some loading of lumber for distant markets. Yet it was here, at Bearskin Neck, that drama so often stirred the calm of remote Cape Ann.

This neck earned its curious name many years before fishermen built a single hut on either side of the narrow, rocky strip of land. In that northeast corner of Cape Ann, then called Sandy Bay, a name, incidentally, assigned ironically to both water and land, it was not just wolves that had terrified the early fishermen. Bears, too, prowled the woodlands then, and preyed upon sheep and cattle. Eventually, the bears became such a nuisance that one day the fishermen agreed they had had enough. Armed with guns, and led by barking dogs, they chased the creatures toward the harbor, to the farthest tip of land, where they, at last, cornered the animals.

In a short time, bearskins draped the rocks at the end of the neck of land, where men spread the skins to dry like their fish. This curious sight caught the eye of other fishermen sailing by, and so amused them that they gave the area its colorful and enduring name—Bearskin Neck.

With bears out of the way for all time, the business of fishing continued, with barrels of fish oil and salt fish often filling to capacity the narrow strip of Bearskin Neck. Still, with no money to improve the rocky soil, the "neck" remained all but impassable for vehicles until 1812, when, once again, some British ships sailed too close to shore. By this time, however, the United States government was in a position to take notice. In an attempt to facilitate its own work of protecting the shoreline, the government hired men and oxen to move some of the boulders, and then to build a passable road over Bearskin Neck.

At the far end of the new road, the government built

a fort on some of the very rocks where fishermen had once dried the bearskins (along with the fish) and where, on a future day, human beings were to take to drying their own skins under the summer sun.

By the time the men had completed the road and the fort, all danger to Cape Ann from British warships had ceased to exist and, once more, the fishermen returned to their fish huts on Bearskin Neck. For there, the fish huts provided all the basic needs for their work, and sometimes families even lived in them.

After building the road, though, it had been but a step to the building of wharves to accommodate the larger vessels being built. The Neck was a logical setting for boat building. The new road also facilitated the hauling of wood from the forests of "oke" trees. Now, the same oak wood was used for houses, as well as for boats. They built larger and larger boats to sail farther and farther away, to haul more and more fish for the increasing markets—in Boston and around the world— and more and more people heard about Cape Ann.

Fish drying and salting, then boat building, inevitably brought about the need for a tavern for thirsty fishermen. The Punch Bowl Tavern, with signs of the punch bowl, went into business on Bearskin Neck, and, for a while longer, the Neck served the needs of the fishermen and their families.

But Bearskin Neck, that stretch of land that had so often been exposed to dangers of wild beasts and war, and always open to fierce storms blowing off the Atlantic, saw only slight changes throughout the 1800s. No paint, plumbing, or electricity as yet compelled the fishermen to change their way of life. Only the sea, as always, created such changes as there were to be made.

Cape Ann was well into the nineteenth century before a Humane Society perceived the need of life-saving equipment for that north side of the Cape, so exposed to every storm that lashed the area. Their concern for water safety resulted in having a life boat stationed at Bearskin Neck. The man qualified as captain of the boat worked on the Neck as a sailmaker. For the next fifty years this man and his volunteers stood by with the life boat whenever they received a call to rescue a crew from a vessel that had been disabled by a storm.

Fishermen volunteers were always at hand, and were usually called upon several times during the winter season to man the life boat with its eight or ten oars of solid ash wood. No fisherman lacked the courage to drive into the crashing surf, and sometimes row several miles toward open sea, regardless of personal danger, to save the life of another fisherman.

Eventually, the United States Coast Guard replaced the efforts of the Humane Society, and the two lots of land once used for the old Humane Society's rescue work, were sold at public auction. The two lots, 16 feet by 35 feet, brought $300 and $275 to the town treasury, a nominal price at the time, 1928, for land that is now valued into the thousands.

The end of the Humane Society was by no means the last act of the drama to be enacted on the tiny stage of Bearskin Neck. For an amazing two-hundred-and-fifty-years, one dramatic incident followed another. After the bearskins had dried to a turn, after huts had been built, after rocks were removed, after a road and fort were built for protection, after salt fish and lumber were loaded onto vessels that sailed to markets around the world, after rescue crews had saved countless lives, after wharves were constructed to accommodate the larger vessels being built, the time had come for this stage to present a new kind of drama.

In a gradual but constant movement, artists had come to take over the fish huts on Bearskin Neck. Although the early artists had no more money than the fishermen, many of them possessed an exceptional talent and could occasionally sell a painting to pay the low rent charges for a fish shack. Almost unnoticed, the barrels of fish oil gave way to the easels and turpentine of the artists, and, though at first artists were only slightly more welcome than the early golddiggers and

The "Round House," studio of Harrison Cady.

pirates had been, they brought undeniable change and color to the unpainted shacks.

For a time, the artists made few changes themselves. They were content to leave the shacks unpainted, and to find their own colors in the weathered wood, but others came to Cape Ann to admire their work, and soon the world came crowding in as far as the ocean on all sides would let them.

Artists who came to paint the quarry rocks, G. T. Margeson and others, could never resist painting the shore rocks about Bearskin Neck as well, nor could they resist taking over the crude fish huts for the low rent they could afford. The fishermen, in their turn, could never resist the ready cash. The Neck, once crowded with barrels of fish oil and salt fish awaiting shipment to Boston, Lisbon, or the West Indies, gradually gave way to the ways of the artists.

Meanwhile, artists quietly sold their paintings from the shops that also served as living quarters, and some stayed on after the summer season, like Margeson, to paint all year long.

Rooms in the new hotels, too, filled to capacity, and at times artists joined forces with the fishermen to resist the great influx of tourists. During one season, for example, objections to tourists reached a point of defiance, much like the fishermen had defied the government in the incident of the whistling buoy off Eastern Point, Gloucester. Signs of the old time squabbling erupted that year on Bearskin Neck. With tourists appearing in ever increasing numbers, those defying the advance of tourism raised their voices still louder. At last, town officials had to admonish them to "settle the family squabble before the guests arrive."

The trouble arose that year over violations of the Lord's Day Act—the Sunday Blue Laws—and a matter of contention for more than fifty years.

"The law is clear," a town official told the shop owners on Bearskin Neck. "You must have a license to open your shops on Sunday."

The shop owners, many of them artists as desperately in need of income as the widows of Dogtown Common, scoffed at the "ridiculous" law. "Is an exhibition of art educational?" they asked, "or simply a commodity for sale like toothpaste and chewing gum?"

It was true, as some said, that artists were now being accused of representing a transient "Bohemian Colony," but by this time many had settled and had become respected members of the community, as well as permanent residents. They claimed, with considerable justification, that the law was aimed, not at them, but at "fly-by-nights" who came to open a shop for a season, and who exhibited "gaudy wares."

While artists attempted to appeal to the expanding tourist trade, there was a genuine fear among them that business was dropping off because of the "honky-tonk" influence. For many, including long-time residents, the new affectation did not fit the old image of Bearskin Neck. Had the ragged waif, they wondered, become a stage performer wearing too much make-up for their taste?

As a result of the quarreling, some artists threatened to move elsewhere and, as they said, "take the tourists with us." This was no idle threat and, if carried out, could have a devastating effect on incomes of the fishermen who rented their huts on the Neck. When the tourists of 1937 arrived, the battle had sky-rocketed to the danger point. Boston newspapers were already publishing cartoons suggesting that "Pretty soon they'll be taking in the scenery!"

It was time for action. One woman, an artist-shop-keeper, responded with the same independent spirit of so many Cape Ann women before her. In her shop, which displayed paintings and marine articles of interest to tourists, she decorated a window with tiny replicas of the *Mayflower*. Then she hung a sign that read "Puritan honky-tonk boats."

When townspeople read her not-so-subtle message they cheered in sympathy, and then they cheered even louder when the town counsel slyly advised her and other offenders how best to defy the law! With so much encouragement, the group of "offenders" threatened to take the matter all the way to the supreme court!

On the Sunday that Patrolman James Quinn set about to enforce the law and close the shops, hundreds turned out "to watch the fun." The law triumphed that day, and for a time the shops closed on Sunday, but shortly new signs of rebellion began to appear in shop windows, some in jest and some in anger.

The same irate female artist-shop owner, who had displayed the "honky-tonk boats," countered the closing with a new sign: "Because of the Sunday Blue Laws we are forbidden to allow anyone to look at pictures on Sunday morning. However, come back at two o'clock."

On Bearskin Neck a subtle shifting of the scenery was under way. A new drama had appeared on stage, created by artists, shopkeepers, and tourists, as well as the fishermen themselves.

22

Bearskin Neck Astir

THE ATLANTIC OCEAN STILL CRASHED IN ON ALL SIDES, still sent its salt spray over the roofs of the huts, never letting the newcomer forget its presence, but the sea-washed, weather-beaten face of Bearskin Neck was about to take on a new look. The hand-craft of the artist replaced the old stage props of barrels of fish oil and salt fish. The boat building that had once spilled out from Bearskin Neck well into the town square, was now all but gone from the scene. But the dramas enacted around the entrance to the Neck, the town square, and on Bearskin Neck itself were not soon forgotten.

One early activity, vital to the town's welfare, was the sinking of the town well in Dock Square. Here, only a few feet from the entrance to Bearskin Neck, where almost as much activity went on as on the Neck itself, the well had been sunk in 1794.

The pump was made of white oak, cut from nearby woods. The well soon became the common source for the town's drinking water. Almost at once, the well became a new gathering place for the fishermen, where they assembled to tell their fish stories as they had for decades in the shacks on Bearskin Neck.

After 1856, when laws put an end to open sales of liquor, men had brought to the well their bottles of bitters, purchased at five cents per bottle and now coveted items for collectors. The bitters were extracts, such as lemon, peppermint, and paregoric; and to the contents of these small bottles thirsty fishermen added a dipperful of cold water from the town pump.

The money to build the well came from public subscription, sponsored by the Reverend Ebenezer Cleveland, who probably had no idea his water project would be turned to such use. The practice of drinking the mixture of water and bitters continued without open objection for over fifty years.

The common pump in the village square was the source of water supply for all homeowners, and was delivered to them and to boat owners, as well, in a delivery wagon. Subscribers paid one penny per bucketful of water, delivered in a wooden barrel (called a jigger) set on the water wagon.

Some Cape Anners who lived in this northeast corner of the Cape, asserted the drinking water was so pure and cold that it was an even greater asset than the ocean in attracting tourists.

"There is magic in the town well," they assured visitors. "Whoever drinks from the town well is compelled to return sometime to drink again."

While the fishermen were always a part of whatever activity went on in the town square and at Bearskin Neck, the women were never far away, and they were always strong and effective. On one memorable occasion they out-performed the fishermen.

The women, stirred to action by over-use of rum at the Punch Bowl Tavern, Dock Square, and at other small shops, planned and carried out a raid to eliminate such a drinking problem from their lives. In one five-hour raid, the group of two-hundred women put an end "for all time" to sales of liquor in Rockport.

After such spirited action, the men of Cape Ann acknowledged that they had tried to "conquer and restrain" the women, but women of Cape Ann were no easier to conquer than the ocean itself. While poets called women "the stone the builders rejected," women refused to be rejected. At one time, after their daring liquor raid, they gathered courage to assert their political views.

23

Woman Power

IN THE YEAR 1700, WHEN CAPE ANN FISHERMEN BOUGHT from the Indians their 10,000 acres of granite ledge, they had assumed "all the rights and profits and privileges thereof." The profits had been slow in coming, and for the rights and privileges the struggle had been constant.

For the women, especially, the "privileges" were almost out of sight, if not entirely out of mind. For a long time, the sole entertainment for women, beyond their fortune telling and palmistry and knitting, had been in going to church. "They knew," as one said, "how to live on little with a cheerful heart." Along with their Bibles, however, women had brought to America their cookbooks, and, while their concoctions of herbs were important for medicinal purposes, baking skills became a matter of special pride.

In those earliest days on Cape Ann, as elsewhere in New England, men gathered in small groups that served them as political parties, while women were still denied the freedom of expressing their political views on a ballot.

Cape Ann women, always resourceful, managed to surmount this oversight by using their unique skills, and soon after the American Revolution they began to influence politics in a way that was dramatic in its simplicity—they baked a cake!

These wives of fishermen, with almost nothing else to boast about, could bake a cake to be proud of, and while they permitted their voting choices to languish at times, they began to practice the persuasive power of the fresh baked cake. Their concoction became known as Election Cake, for it was baked only once a year, for the annual June election of a governor, and was served all day to politicians and campaign workers.

The cake, of course, was no ordinary cake, nor was Election Day an ordinary day. Both involved the entire family and both required weeks of preparation. This day of celebration called for speeches and parades, feasting and merrymaking, as well as serving the raised cake delicacy, Election Cake.

Long before Election Day, women began to assemble the necessary ingredients for their cakes. Though the

Election Cake.

recipes varied somewhat, some calling for one egg and others for as many as seven, all recipes required the exotic spices that sailor husbands now brought from distant ports, and all required the long hours of preparation.

With all ingredients ready, and each measured out in pounds or "half-handfuls" instead of by cupsful, the housewife was ready to begin her cake by raising a batch of soft yeast dough. As prepared yeast did not appear on the American market until 1865, Cape Ann housewives before that time learned to make do with whatever was available to them, often a rye grain softened with wine, or with molasses and sugar, and left in the sun to ferment.

In colonial times, cakes were nearly always started with this dough base, then mixed with a cake batter. This simple bread-dough mixture, commonly baked in country ovens, was often confused with the richer and more elegant creation that emerged from brick ovens as Election Cake.

Some old houses had two brick ovens, even now visible in some Cape Ann homes, for the quantity of cooking necessary for the large families. These brick-lined cavities were perfect for the long, slow baking of Election Cake.

After the ingredients were assembled, the fruit chopped, and all mixed together, then a time allowed for rising, still interminable hours remained for the baking, while for days the sweet aroma of those round bread-dough confections wafted through Cape Ann homes.

When the cakes emerged from the ovens, they

looked exactly as the recipes had promised—high, round, crusty, dotted with raisins, and usually gleaming with thin slices of citron. After the cake had cooled, the final step was to drizzle over all a sugary topping, called treacle. On the long awaited day, the neighbors crowded in to the too small kitchens to sample this extraordinary food that had taken weeks to prepare.

There is no record of how many election tides rose and fell with Election Cake, but when Cape Ann housewives served the high-rise spongy cake, tangy with fruits and spices and filled with raisins, the kitchen propaganda system could scarcely fail. In any case, hopeful politicians who came to sip a cup of steaming coffee and munch a slice of Election Cake must have felt repaid for their day's efforts.

Eventually, the cake became so well known all over New England that small bakeries rose to fame, as well. Around the year 1800, cookbooks began to print versions of the recipe, but inexperienced cooks soon found this cake was not something that could be whipped up on short notice, and few had the patience or the determination of those early women politicians.

In one respect, at least, the baked cake proved to be a master stroke; not only did it tempt the palate of adult politicians, but it delighted young Cape Ann voters of the future. School boys, calling on the old sea magic in place of the coins they never had, rated Election Cake a special treat. Soon after dawn on Election Day, the boys raced each other from their fishing dories to homes or to a nearby bakery, offering a fresh-caught haddock in exchange for a piece of the delectable Election Cake.

"The recipe is always right," proclaimed an ad in an old Cape Ann cookbook. "If the cake fails, perhaps it is the cook!"

ELECTION CAKE

1 pint milk	1 tsp. cinnamon
1 yeast cake	½ tsp.nutmeg
1 tsp. salt	4 well beaten eggs
½ cup lukewarm water	2 cups raisins
5–6 cups flour	½ cup sliced citron
1 cup butter	figs and other fruit as desired
2 cups brown sugar	molasses for a glaze

Prepare soft dough with first five ingredients and allow time to rise double in bulk. After several hours, cream butter and brown sugar. Add spices and the beaten eggs. Combine with yeast mixture. Flour the raisins, citron, figs, dates and other fruit and add to mixture. Let dough rise again until light, then cut the dough down and shape into two large baking pans, round if available, about ⅔ full. Let rise again until light. Bake in moderate oven, 350 degrees. Glaze with treacle (molasses) and return to oven for five minutes to set glaze, or drip a thin icing over all.

24

Catering to the Tourist

THE DAYS WERE PAST WHEN WOMEN MUST RAISE THEIR own dough for baking; the days were gone for the fishermen to chop their bait with a hatchet; the dream of the early fishermen to "fill every cove that hugged the Cape Ann shore" had been fulfilled. So many strangers now came to Cape Ann that often houses had to be moved to make room for families to build more homes.

From the need for more houses the practice of house-moving developed, and houses were on the move all summer long. Indeed, the city of Gloucester appointed a house-mover-in-chief. The fact that the mover was also the mayor of the city afforded him certain privileges necessary to moving houses. With the power of his office, he assumed the right to attach ropes to trees along the route the house was to be moved, to trim

Dock Square, 1909.

branches wherever necessary to allow smooth passage, and even to drive heavy iron spikes into asphalt surfaces, even though recently paved!

All this house moving, needless to say, caused acute traffic problems. One house being moved from Bearskin Neck was so delayed that night closed in before it reached its destination. As a result, the family, including three small girls, spent the night sleeping in their house on stilts, set in the center of Dock Square!

The habit of house moving came to an end with all the natural progress taking place. As more electric wires were strung about the Cape, they not only became more expensive to remove as each house rolled by, but housewives launched vehement objections to having electric power turned off without notice.

Dock Square, c. 1975.

Electricity was not only a new commodity to be cherished by the housewife, but it was also an accommodation to the tourist. In one section of Cape Ann, an area of new summer cottages, electric bulbs were turned on for the summer people, then removed when all cottages were vacated at the end of the summer season.

Such "catering" to the tourist was not always approved of, but one Cape Ann woman developed her own unique style of welcome for the newcomer.

25

Susie's Special Welcome

SUSIE PETTINGILL WAS BORN IN 1874 AND WAS, AS ONE writer described her, "hard-working, a good neighbor, with great independence in so small a frame."

Susie was as proud as many Cape Anners of her British ancestry, perhaps prouder, for she could boast of ancestral ties with the royal House of Windsor. It was her ties with Cape Ann, however, that made Susie's life a vibrant melody, a song of love that expressed her affection for neighbors, as well as strangers.

One day, when a summer visitor remarked that she missed her home garden and wished she had a place to "dig" while on vacation, Susie replied without hesitation, "You can dig in my garden as much as you like," and the summer guest grew a fine garden of vegetables on Susie's free soil.

Except for her English grandfather, who was a Baptist minister, Susie's family were all seamen. Her father, uncles, and cousins worked at the business of sailing blocks of granite down the coast, on a stone sloop they had patriotically named the America. One day, as they sailed from Knowlton's Wharf with a load of granite blocks, one of the boys spied a mast floating behind Thachers Island. "From some millionaire's yacht, probably," he speculated, and the boys towed it into Rockport harbor. From the harbor they managed to tug it home and set it up in Susie's yard to use for a flagpole. For these seamen, the rigging of a flagpole was as easy as rigging a vessel, and in a short time the musically gifted young Susie had found a new use for another piece of flotsam from the sea.

Susie sang from morning 'til night. She sang in the church choir and she played the church organ with professional skill. "The whole family grew up singing," she often said. Now, with an American flag to sing to, Susie and her family established a daily ritual of singing the "Star Spangled Banner" at daybreak. This habit Susie maintained to the end of her long life, after all her family was gone, and she continued the daily practice of raising the flag and singing the national anthem through all four verses.

Susie's music led her to the poetry of the Bible, and,

Susie Pettingill's house and candy shop on Cleaves Street.

after her daily concert at the flagpole, she read her daily message from the Bible; but these activities were only the beginning of her busy day.

In the front of her house, Susie kept a penny candy store for children of the neighborhood, long after that kind of shop went out of style. Her house and shop were a three-minute walk to the beach, and at midday she took her daily swim "to keep in trim." Since she must take the short walk along Main Street, her modesty forced her to lengthen her bathing suit with a ruffle; and for good measure she added long stockings to her outfit. Older residents recalled that she had been a graceful skater in her youth, as well as a swimmer of ability. After her daily swims she weeded and pruned her garden of roses. At sunset it was time to close the candy shop and lower the flag.

For seventy-five years Susie carried on for her father and uncles as she raised the flag on her forty-foot flag-pole and sang the national anthem. After nearly eight decades, when the flagpole began to show the decay of age, Susie worried that her singing of the national anthem was about to come to an end; that the flag would no longer wave from that sea-gift to her family—the ship mast flagpole.

Susie need not have worried for town officials were as concerned as she was, and soon had plans under way to replace the decaying flagpole. The population of the entire town, includng summer visitors, had no intention of missing Susie's daily ceremony. Somehow, the neces-sary funds appeared to buy whatever pipe and fittings the work required, and men in the department of public works erected a flagpole just in time to say "Merry Christmas" to Susie in 1959.

Susie's music and her patriotism carried outside Cape Ann, all the way to the White House in Washing-ton. From President Eisenhower she received Flag Day greetings and a personal letter, which she cherished to the end of her days. Six years later, when she was 92, Susie's flag flew at half mast for her final performance.

Although Susie had often confessed jokingly that she had little use for "cats, dogs, and men," she had found room in her heart not only for her neighbors but for the many tourist-strangers who came her way.

26

More Signs of Welcome

THE STRANGERS NOW FILLING THE GUEST HOUSES, INNS, and hotels that sprang up to accommodate them came to study works of the artists and to listen to the ageless secrets of the ocean.

Tourism began to move on its own momentum and, with competition, outdoor advertising inevitably came to Cape Ann. This method of attracting the tourist, although accepted with reluctance to this day, and often considered unnecessary, was here to stay.

Many Cape Anners disapproved of the old English custom of hanging out a wooden sign, called "puffing," since it was viewed as boasting. Nevertheless, one landlady had tried the scheme in the earliest days of Cape Ann.

That enterprising landlady of the eighteenth century peered through her window at her first tourist, a sea captain, who had over-imbibed with rum after a long sea voyage. After disembarking, he approached the only candle-lit house within walking distance of the harbor. A wooden sign indicated the house was a haven for weary travelers, and the captain yelled a greeting, but the landlady, noting his condition, refused to admit him.

"Go 'way," she shouted through her locked door.

The captain, furious at being turned away from the only rooming house then available, quickly unsheathed a hatchet from his belt and, with one powerful stroke, slashed the welcome sign in half. Then, stumbling and grumbling, he returned to sleep yet another night on his vessel.

The sign on the post hung broken and limp for many months, until a winter storm finished what the objectionable guest had begun. Meanwhile, some of the neighbors hinted that the landlady had left the broken sign as a lure, as well as a warning, to other travelers.

If, however, that first shattered sign hung in pieces to lure the tourists on the south side of the Cape, soon another sign, equally as eye-catching, attracted travelers on the north side of the Cape.

In Pigeon Cove, where hotel accommodations were more plentiful, Captain Daniel Wheeler "kept tavern."

First summer boarding house, The Old Tavern, in Pigeon Cove.

This tavern was not only a way to accommodate over-nighters, but was also a gathering place for sociability and sometimes "a mug of flip" passed around the group for the price of a "button," or fourpence.

At Captain Wheeler's tavern, another early sign post was a conversation piece for years. This sign, carved in the shape of an elm tree, could not help but attract city dwellers, although only the owner's name on the sign indicated it was a "public house."

The Wheeler Tavern, now located in the center of Pigeon Cove traffic, was then, in 1805, surrounded by pasture land, and on the south edge of the property stood a gate that, when closed, separated the north village from the south village (Rockport). From this point, also, it was a short walk across "the beach," which, in more recent years, has slumbered under the Cape Ann Tool Company.

Over the years, the small business sign became the beckoning finger to the traveler, and as each new season approached, freshly painted "vacancy" signs swung with expectancy. Inevitably, some permanent residents began to wonder about the newcomers, as had their ancestors, and to question whether the signs should be hung at all, such hordes of tourists streamed in anyway.

Nevertheless, the signs became the spokesmen for the seaside communities of Cape Ann, usually expressive and often eloquent. At the time of that first tourist sign, shattered by the old sea captain, there was only one sign, one signpost, one rooming house. Soon, however, other rooming houses and taverns opened for the transient business. The Wheeler Tavern, and the now historic Punch Bowl Tavern on Bearskin Neck, with its sign of the punch bowl, invited merrymakers who "with frolic and mirth drove dull care away." (In recent years no taverns have been permitted in Rockport, therefore no liquor signs exist.)

Eventually, town officials came to realize, with impressive foresight, that even small signs could be as offensive to the eye as the roadside billboard; that

Signs showing good taste and artistry of merchants and signmakers.

although the signs spoke for the business community, their size and artistry must be kept within modest bounds.

More than two centuries had passed since that first tourist sign appeared on Cape Ann, but under the growing influence of artists, signs became more numerous and colorful.

Outside of the villages, on the early New England highways, scarcely a sign marred the landscape. The few that did appear only served to confuse one traveler who explained to a tourist even more bewildered than himself, "If you are heading north, you follow the blue and white signs to Maine, the green and white signs to New Hampshire, and," he added,"the safest way to keep from getting lost is to keep the ocean on the right."

The ocean had never stopped giving directions to Cape Ann and, while history and long custom gave shape to the imagination, the sign makers tried to balance business needs with the new aesthetic considerations. On sign posts outside rooming houses, the new gift shops and the restaurants, a gilded sea captain, carved in wood, scanned the ocean with his binoculars. With a green parrot perched on his shoulder, he joined other artistic creations—a Yankee clipper ship with a constant wind filling its sails; a dolphin; a whale; a lobster; sea creatures, all carved in wood to stir the interest of the curious traveler.

Business names, too, became significant to Cape Ann, as had rock names so many years before the travelers came. Such varied names as Rocky Shores, and Boulder Top rivaled The Beaches. Although most names suggested nearness to the sea, there were also a Paper House, a Witch House, and a House of Glass. But for the tourist who preferred sea names above all others, there was the Seaward, Sea Crest, Sea View, Sea Shell, and even the Sea Gull.

Not all the signs, however, expressed imagination, not all were artistic, but few were gaudy or obtrusive. Taken as a whole, and conforming as they must to a legal limitation of three square feet, they displayed a restraint that was directed not only by the town by-laws, but by the personalities of the owners, as well.

Some signs revealed a pared-to-the-bone simplicity of the New England innkeeper, stating merely the street and number, as Seven South Street or Twenty-three King Street, but all these signs of the tourist trade served well to mirror the offerings of local merchants. For three centuries, imaginative signs became the kind of welcome that Cape Ann learned to extend to the stranger-guest, though one day the Chamber of Commerce and Board of Trade discovered a unique way to extend an even warmer welcome. They chose to "say it with flowers." They ordered a structure of iron to be hand-wrought by a skilled local artisan; then they attached this framework to parking meters. The final step was to hang baskets of flowing ivy geranium and lantana high over the heads of pedestrians, permitting the pink and lavender bloom to drape gracefully over the offensive parking meters.

The baskets of blossoms, in addition to the signs on wood, spread a mute welcome from the old fishermen to the new travelers on Cape Ann. Cape Ann had finally abandoned her distain of visitors, and now began searching for ways to lure newcomers to her coves, to view the works of art she so proudly displayed.

27

Time for Culture

BY THE YEAR 1939, THE TOWN THAT HAD ONCE BEEN SHORT on culture suddenly found itself with more works of art than it knew what to do with. James Quinn, the same police officer who had settled the squabble on Bearskin Neck, now conceived an idea to solicit paintings from all the best artists and hang them in the new fire-police station under construction in Rockport.

The new building, constructed of native granite blocks with $80,000 of W.P.A funds, was to house thirty-nine fine paintings and one sculpture, without a single refusal by the artists. Jimmie's zeal, however, outdistanced that of the building contractors and the paintings were ready to be hung before completion of the building. For two weeks, the valuable works of art were stacked in a vacant shop to await a future hanging.

The "new" Police Station, 1939.

Boston newspapers flaunted headlines of the art to be hung in a fire–police station, and Cape Ann once more became the subject of good-natured ridicule.

"The last word in jails," reporters wrote. And then to dramatize further, "Art in a Calaboose." One reported that there was "Landscape, Seascape, and Escape" at the "Rockport Cop House."

Nevertheless, when the paintings were finally hung in the new building, the *Boston Herald* conceded it was the only art gallery in the country to be opened 365 days a year and 24 hours a day!

Police officer James Quinn, c. 1940.

James Quinn's dream to "lend a fitting cultural background for the town" had succeeded, and Cape Ann was at last in the public eye, willing or not. Still, amid all the pageantry of Cape Ann's coves and villages, the greatest curtain raiser of all was yet to be staged.

28

First Prize

WHETHER EVENTS ON CAPE ANN WERE OF WORLD SIGNI-
ficance, such as the landing of the cable in 1884, or
merely of community interest, like the sinking of the
town pump or moving a house for a fisherman's family,
the sea was always there to remind Cape Anners of their
past.

No matter where the houses or hotels were built,
neither visitor nor resident ever slept more than three
miles from the sea. Along the shore, first the boarding
houses, then summer hotels, then the newer homes
appeared, all within sight and sound of the ocean. At
Pigeon Cove, about the time Ralph Waldo Emerson
visited Cape Ann (1855), forty houses spread over the
farmland and rock ledges, all of them built with a panoramic view of the ocean. The Atlantic was never for

a moment out of the minds of Cape Anners or their guests.

Nor were the early fishermen ever forgotten. Though the stone cutters came, then the artists, then the curious tourists, the fishermen's shacks remained as if to remind the world of Cape Ann's origin. It is not surprising, then, that it was the shacks, those lean-tos without paint, that especially caught the attention of artists who saw in them Cape Ann's primitive beauty.

One of these structures, now called "Motif Number One," is the crowned queen of Cape Ann fish houses and, though the title may sound more roguish than regal, the queen does, in reality, wear a triple crown.

The story of the simple wooden structure, standing alone on its granite base in Rockport Harbor, is the three part saga of a transformation from commoner to queen. From the humblest of beginnings, as an unpainted fish hut designed for nothing more than the storing of fish, bait, and fishing gear, the little house became a symbol of a community's future, as well as its past. Among the dozens of fish shacks that cluster about Cape Ann's coves, where pirates once sought shelter, there is no longer any doubt that Motif Number One wears the crown.

The shack, long claimed by fishermen, still serves as a store-house for lobster pots and bait, and as a resting place, too, for soaring seagulls. But its position as an artist's subject is its crowning jewel.

Its history as a model for painters began in 1862, when the railroad brought the curious, many of them artists. They came to paint the always changing sea and the crude little fish house in the harbor at Rockport.

After Gilbert Tucker Margeson arrived from Boston and began to send and receive messages by Western Union wire, other artists followed, attracted by the simplicity of the structure at the edge of the harbor.

More and more visitors began to reconstruct the primitive beauty on their canvasses until, one day, an artist who had actually taken up residence in the building, along with the fishing gear, realized his shelter had become the most popular subject of all for his fellow artists to paint. Repeating, half in jest, the words brought from France by his contemporary artist, Lester Hornby, the tenant-owner uttered the name that was to remain for posterity: "It's the Number One Motif!"

Shortly after the house received its name, something happened to change the world's perception of the little house for all time. The unlikely city of Detroit, Michigan, played a small but significant role in the history of the queen of Cape Ann fish houses.

The year was 1932. Detroit was host that year to the American Legion Convention, to which two Rockport men were sent as delegates. Dr. Earl Green and Mr. A. Carl Butman, a businessman, had watched the convention's parade of floats through Detroit streets that September day and had returned to their hotel weary but inspired.

"Next year, in Chicago," Dr. Green said, "why not enter a float in the parade?" A float, they dreamed, would advertise their own sleepy seacoast village of Rockport that was then deep in the country's economic depression. Their dreams soared, as dreams of Cape Ann had soared for generations, and these two men envisioned a bonanza for a village that had rarely seen prosperity. Their thoughts flew 900 miles eastward and settled like a seagull on a solitary fish shack back home; a fish hut standing humble and wave-splashed at the end of a pier, an unpretentious structure used mainly for stored bait and lobster gear, and, of course, as a way-station for the ever-present seagulls.

Their dream of a parade float, a replica of the familiar fish house, became more real once they returned home. The idea, born in an inland city where the personnel in any auto plant exceeded the entire population of Rockport many times over, caught the instant enthusiasm of the folks back in the village.

In a short time, the fish house with the faded shingles became a symbol of the town's age-old fishing

Motif Number One.

industry. At the same time, it represented the new colony of artists that had become such an integral part of the Cape. In addition, and most importantly, it gave promise of awakening a slumbering tourist industry.

During the months that followed the dream in Detroit, a model began to take shape, a model of the fish house fashioned to scale and as authentic as volunteer artisans could make it. Local artists lent their talented hands, and the fishermen helped, as well. The project soon required the services of a skilled ship builder, too, for the masts and booms for the four tiny boats moored realistically at the make-believe wharf. Others were called upon to do the iron work and to make the netting for the rigging of sails and lobster pots, giving it as much authenticity as possible.

The model, built with exceptional realism, measured twenty-seven feet long, eight-and-a-half feet wide, and twelve and a half feet to the tip of the masts. For a final perfect detail, the chimney and masts were hinged as a precaution against any low bridges the entourage might encounter on the trip to Chicago.

During that Depression summer of 1933, family income may have been minimal, but there was little unemployment in Rockport. Members of the American Legion, boatmen, and artists all worked together. By September, construction of the float was complete. Only three final tasks remained: to load the structure with great care onto a truck chassis; to round up the men who were to serve as escort to Chicago; and to take a "dry run" around town for a final approval by the towns-people.

The group finally set off on the five-day journey to Chicago amid tooting horns and shouting well-wishers. The town's single police officer, James Quinn, rode his motorcycle and, incidentally, set the world's long distance record of that time for a police motorcycle escort.

"All day and into the night I'd keep going," Jim

related after the trip, "until I'd find a suitable place to stop to eat or to put up for the night."

No hotel rooms had been reserved in advance this time, for inside the float, bunks were concealed for the men to sleep enroute.

"Often we stopped in a town square," said Jim. "Then we'd hook up cables to spotlight the float, and at night it looked just like a painting!"

The little group moved slowly westward toward Chicago. One tire blow-out delayed them in Springfield, Massachusetts, but for most of the trip they proceeded at 35 or 40 miles per hour. They traveled through the Berkshire Mountains, to South Bend, Indiana, and on to Chicago. At the same time, a few Cape Anners made the trip by train at a cost of $20.05 for a round-trip ticket.

Jim Quinn escorted the float safely into Chicago and guided it to a parking lot at the Navy pier, near Lake Michigan. They arrived in time for a day of rest before the Monday parade.

The parade wound on all day, and, as soon as the Rockport float had passed the judges' stand, the driver, with Jim in his position as escort, slipped out of Chicago and headed home. He left without waiting to hear the name of the prize-winning float.

Somewhere along the way, as the group headed east, the news reached them that their float, in competition with 199 other floats from around the country, had won first prize! Then, all along the route homeward, reception committees welcomed the Motif Number One, now truly the number one prize winner from Rockport, Massachusetts.

The prize for the float was $100 dollars, but the tourist value now of the little fish house in the harbor at Rockport was incalculable. The fame of the fish house spread faster than the group could travel, and when the float reached home to the applause of proud Cape Anners, the publicity that followed soon brought more glory to the real fish house than the two men in Detroit could have dreamed of. Then, as its new fame spread, plans developed to protect and preserve Motif Number One. Homage must now be paid to the queen of fish houses.

The emergence of the fish house as a model for artists to paint became the first star in the queen's crown. The second star was the prize-winning replica that brought fame to the village and the house, itself. The third star in the triple crown brought an entirely new aspect to the old fish hut. Unfortunately, this third part of the crown started out on a negative note.

In the course of planning for the restoration of the aging structure, a legal snag all but terminated plans for the preservation. Once again, it took the artists to

Float depicting Motif No. 1.

realize the first step was a protective coat of paint. Now very practical questions arose. Who owned the shack? Who would paint it? Who, indeed, would pay the cost of a coat of paint?

Arguments flared on Main Street, in the art galleries, and among the boat owners; arguments that swirled in sometimes heated, but more often good-natured controversy.

One day, in the midst of the arguments, the artist-owner came forward and made himself known. Having no further use for the shack, and fearful of undesirable exploitation of his beloved village, he offered to sell the shack to the town for the sum of $3,500. This offer seemed a fair price at the time, but then there was the next question: What would the villagers do with the fish house if they bought it? With no good answer ensuing, the famous model went into storage, while twelve years and World War II slipped into history.

It was 1945, during a lengthy annual town meeting, that the subject of what to do with Motif Number One came up again. Tempers flared anew at the prospect of further delays, while attentive listeners repeated the old question, " What will the town do with it once it is purchased?"

The town attorney presented a legal snag that nearly quashed the entire proposal. "No funds can be spent for a building," he proclaimed, "that serves no public purpose."

The verbal battle went on until voters had exhausted all their arguments. In the end, a woman artist, Ruth Spoor, arose from her stiff-backed bench and brought the discussion to a close. As heads turned toward her to listen, she spoke with a gentle persuasion as sure as the incoming tide.

"Let us," she proposed, "make this now famous building a memorial to our men and women who have served in the armed services."

For a moment snow boots ceased their restless shuffling. Heads began to nod with approval. Sporadic clapping gave way to tumultuous applause. There was now no question about its use. In the minds of all, this was certainly "public purpose." Then Rockport citizens reached into their pockets to buy and preserve the building that had come to represent so many interests that all who gazed upon it could affectionately lay claim to it. No monument ever inspired greater pride of ownership.

With town purchase now assured, once more artists came forward and volunteer hands set to work. Again, those artists with distinguished names selected and mixed paint with as much care as for their finest professional works of art. In a short time the faded little hut stood revealed to the world in its splendid new coat. Painted in the color the artists chose for it—"A warm red mixture without glare"—with its sides bedecked by the fishermen, all unaware of their own unique artistry, with hand-carved buoys of rainbow colors. Cinderella's tattered garments had magically changed to royal robes befitting a queen.

At last, more tourists came to Cape Ann than the early fishermen could have possibly imagined. First they came by the hundreds, then by the thousands, to gaze upon the queen, and to search for the beauty in the simple lines of the fish hut as revealed to them by the trained eyes of the artists.

All the mystery of the sea, all the magic of the early

witches of Dogtown, all the vision of the first fishermen, as well as the men in Detroit, clung to this one unpretentious shack as tourists came to ponder its long and eventful route from commoner to queen.

Amid all the admiration, the queen stood alone, as queens often do, and as wives of fishermen had done long before. While waves washed her feet of stone, while swirling winds and seagulls whispered to her the many secrets of the sea, she waited in her quiet dignity.

Storms, however, often mar a queen's serenity. The sea plays no favorites, but treats alike the commoner and the queen; and the familiar tragedies that had always stalked the fishing vessels of Cape Ann, lurked offshore to haunt the queen.

29

Blown Away—and Back

DURING THE NIGHT OF FEBRUARY 6, 1978, A SNOW STORM such as no one then living on Cape Ann had ever witnessed, battered the harbors and beat upon the aging and fragile queen. When the first tide receded in the early morning hours, it left the famous fish house weakened and staggering on its feet of stone.

By Tuesday, February 7, a new tide due at mid-morning was expected to surge even higher than the tide of the night before. Villagers waited anxiously for word of the queen's safety. Those whose anxiety led them to venture into the swirling snow to keep a fearful eye on the queen, watched in apprehension as the sea crashed again and again around her feet. At this time of year there were few tourists, but townspeople continued to gather in the midst of nature's fury, frozen particles of snow stinging their faces and blurring their vision. Small groups peered toward the harbor, as other watchful Cape Anners had gazed out to sea for generations, from Dock Square, from Bearskin Neck, and from every wharf near enough to view the latest drama to unfold in a Cape Ann harbor. They waited, knowing in their hearts that nothing could save her; knowing they were powerless, as fishermen had always been, against the relentless fury of the sea.

"She's gone," someone shouted above the howling wind, and bystanders peering into the storm looked once more and turned away. The proud queen, unable to keep her footing against the powerful tide water, washed off her stone base and crumpled helplessly in a heap of sodden kindling.

Disasters to Cape Ann were as familiar as old sea myths, and while curious visitors streamed in to view the damage left in the wake of the storm, and to lament that the famous fish house was gone forever, most failed to reckon with Cape Ann's past.

The past was always the sea, and Cape Ann still received her directives from the sea. This time the message from the sea was unmistakable; it was time to build a new and stronger fish house.

Within hours, even before the storm's damage had been assessed, talk began of rebuilding Motif Number

THE TRAGEDY
AND TRIUMPH OF
MOTIF NO. 1

The tragedy and triumph of Motif No. 1.

One. A committee of volunteers formed to consider plans for reconstruction, of setting the queen back on her throne. The trouble with the old shack, they said, was that the early fishermen had little concern if tides and storms did knock down a fishing shack or two. The sea was always the master and the tides must be obeyed. A fish shack was easy to replace.

In August 1978, seven months after the great storm, workmen poured a new foundation on top of the old granite base. This time the queen must be fitted to sturdier shoes!

30

Nature's Plan Complete

THOUGH THE WORLD NOW TRAVELS TO CAPE ANN'S DOOR; though boats crowd the coves and harbors as the early fishermen predicted, Cape Ann's groping need for human contact goes on. Where once only that first watery highway brought the curious, three additional routes now lead travelers to Cape Ann.

The "cut" bridge was long ago made safe for all vehicles. The railroad brought first the artist, then the vacationer, and another century saw the building of a modern bridge over the Annisquam River, at last bringing as many motor vehicles as Cape Ann could hold.

Amid these changes the sea goes on, molding and moving the rocks like chess men, as it has for thousands of years, remaining the conqueror, never the conquered;

Remains of the home of Helvi and Arthur Olson near Pigeon Cove Harbor.

always the voice that commands and the finger that points the way.

Though scientists probe the ocean's mysteries as never before, though children seek their origins from the ancient sea animals, answers elude modern searchers, even as they eluded the early fishermen.

If there is a magic that brings the world to Cape Ann's door, perhaps the magic lies in the ancient lesson of the sea as it was taught by the fishermen. "Watch every step. Never move forward without first looking back."

Cape Ann's backward look reflects the great gifts of

The storm of February 6–7, 1978, left debris piled in the rear of the Cape Ann Tool Company.

the ice and the rocks and the sea. To some, these may be humble gifts; but for many more, they are the gifts that Nature planned thousands of years ago for Tragabigzanda.

BIBLIOGRAPHY

Ambler, Edward J., *Know Cape Ann*. Manchester, Mass.:
    North Shore Press, 1937.

Babson, John J., *History of Gloucester*. Gloucester, Mass.:
    Proctor Bros., 1860.

Babson and Saville, *Cape Ann: A Tourist Guide*. Rockport,
    Mass.: Sandy Bay Historical Society, 1936.

Chamberlin and Williams, *The Old Castle*. Pigeon Cove,
    Mass.: Village Improvement Society, 1939.

Cooley, John L., *Rockport Sketchbook*. Rockport, Mass.:
    Rockport Art Association, 1965.

Copeland and Rogers, *Saga of Cape Ann*. Freeport, Maine:
    Bond Wheelwright, 1960.

Early, Eleanor, *And This Is Boston*. Boston, Mass.: Hough-
    ton, Mifflin, 1930.

Gott, Lemuel, *History of Rockport*. Rockport, Mass.: *Rockport Review*, 1888.

Gould, R. T., *Case of the Sea Serpent*. New York: G. P. Putnam, 1934.

Hawthorne, Hildegarde, *Old Seaport Towns of New England*. New York: Dodd, Mead, 1916.

Hubbard, William, *General History of New England to 1680*. Boston: Little, Brown, 1843.

Johnson, Clifton, *Highways and Byways of New England*. New York: Macmillan, 1915.

Josselyn, John, *An Account of Two Voyages to New England*. boston: William Veazie, 1865.

Kenny, Herbert A., *Cape Ann: Cape America*. Philadelphia and New York: Lippincott, 1971.

Leonard, Henry C., *Pigeon Cove and Vicinity*. Boston: F. A. Searle, 1873.

Mann, Charles A., *The Story of Dogtown*. Gloucester: Proctor Bros., 1896 and 1906.

Manning, *Manning Papers*. Rockport: Dr. N. A. Hooper Collection.

Marshall, J. W., *John White Marshall Papers*. Rockport, Mass.: Sandy Bay Historical Society. (*See also* History of Essex County.)

Massachusetts Historical Society, Collections. Boston: Essex Institute.

Morison, Samuel Eliot, *History of Maritime Massachusetts*.

Parsons, Eleanor C., *Hannah and Hatchet Gang*. Canaan, New Hampshire: Phoenix Publishing, 1975.

Parsons, Kitty, *Ballad of Dogtown Common*. Gloucester: Self-published, 1936.

Parsons, Kitty, *Gloucester Ballads, (Sea Serpent)*. Gloucester: Cape Ann Ticket & Label, 1946.

Perley, Sidney, *Indian Land Titles*. Salem, Mass.: Essex Institute.

Pool, Ebenezer, *Papers*. Rockport: Sandy Bay Historical Society.

Proctor Brothers, *The Fishermen's Own Book*. Gloucester: compiled by Proctor Brothers.

Proctor, George H., *The Fishermen Memorial Record Book*. Gloucester: Proctor Brothers, 1873.

Reynolds, J., *Peter Gott, the Cape Ann Fisherman*. Gloucester: Proctor Brothers, 1856.

Shaler, Nathaniel S., *Geology of Cape Ann*. Washington, D.C.: U.S. Government Survey Report, 1888.

Smith, John, *A Description of New England*. London; Boston reprint: Humphrey Lownes, 1616 and William Veazie, 1865.

Smith, Sylvanus, *Fisheries of Cape Ann*. Gloucester: Press of Gloucester Times, 1915.

Solley and Dummer, *Alluring Rockport*. Manchester, Mass.: North Shore Press, 1924.

Stockton, Frank, *Buccaneers and Pirates Off Our Coast*. 1934.

er, J. Wingate, *The Landing at Cape Ann*. Boston: Gould and Lincoln, 1854.

Verrill, A. Hyatt, *Along New England Shores*. New York: Putnam, 1936.

Verrill, A. Hyatt, *The Real Story of the Pirate*. New York: Appleton-Century, 1923.

Winthrop, John, *History of New England, 1630–1649*. Boston: Little, Brown, 1853. Reprint by James Savage, Massachusetts Historical Society.

Young, Alexander, *Chronicles*. Boston: Little, Brown. Reprint of 1846 edition by Genealogical Publications, Baltimore.